HAUNTED
MARION, OHIO

HAUNTED
MARION, OHIO

JOSHUA SIMPKINS

Haunted
America

Published by Haunted America
A Division of The History Press
Charleston, SC 29403
www.historypress.net

First published 2011

Manufactured in the United States

ISBN 978.1.60949.235.9

Library of Congress Cataloging-in-Publication Data

Simpkins, Josh.
Haunted Marion, Ohio / Josh Simpkins.
p. cm.
Includes bibliographical references (p.   ).
ISBN 978-1-60949-235-9
1. Ghosts--Ohio--Marion. 2. Haunted places--Ohio--Marion. I. Title.
BF1472.U6S56 2011
133.109771'514--dc23
2011025742

CONTENTS

ACKNOWLEDGEMENTS

I would like to extend my thanks to the following people for their help and support. Although I haven't mentioned them directly in this book, they were all instrumental in its development. Tom White, Gale Martin and Mary Gross at the Marion County Historical Society; Dawn McCleery, Whitney Mahle, Kathy Stroupe and the rest of the reference and circulation staff at the Marion Public Library; and Tom Graser at the *Marion Star*, for generously allowing me to reprint some photos.

INTRODUCTION

This book began as a conversation I had a few years ago with my nephew, Seth. He was still in high school at the time and could hardly wait to get out of Marion. He asked me where I'd live if I could live anywhere in the world. When I told him Marion, he couldn't believe it. "Of all the places in the world, you'd live *here*? Why?!" Besides the obvious fact that the majority of my friends and family live in Marion, I said that it's the only place where I really feel at ease. I also told him that of all the cities I've lived in—including a few abroad—I find Marion the most interesting.

Later, I thought about what I'd said to Seth. Is Marion really an interesting place? It's not that I think Marion would strike any out-of-towners as particularly mind-blowing if they were simply passing through it. But for someone like myself who grew up here, I feel as though I know Marion in ways that only someone with real roots here can ever know it.

And what I know is that Marion is a town with some good stories. While some of these stories end up in the local news, often the most compelling stories are the ones that travel by word of mouth. These are the ones people tell one another in bars over beers or in churches after service—the stories people share in the bleachers at ballgames and on the factory floors.

This book, then, is a collection of some of those stories, albeit ones with a decidedly macabre bent. (What can I say? I wanted the stories about Marion to have a common subject, and since I have an interest in the odd, the scary and the supernatural, this was as good a theme as any.) So, during the summer of 2008, I began collecting stories, both through doing research at the library and through simply talking to people around town.

When I had about a half-dozen stories, I bought the domain www.spookymarion.com, put together a website and put the stories online. The site began getting a decent number of hits. Encouraged, I tried to update it on a semiregular basis. In the fall of 2010, a guy named Joe Gartrell from The History Press contacted me to ask if I was interested in writing a book on Marion that would be part of the publisher's "Haunted America" series. I readily agreed.

While I'm rambling on in this introduction, I'd like to take this opportunity to make a few things clear.

First, in the course of writing this book, a lot of people have questioned me about my own attitude concerning the supernatural. While I believe in keeping an open mind, I have never seen anything even remotely supernatural—no ghosts, no bumps in the night and no disembodied voices. This doesn't mean that I simply dismiss other people's experiences as nonsense—I've just never had any myself.

I've also done my best to document the sources of the information I've used to write this book. This information comes from both archival research and interviews. The decision about whether those sources are *credible* is something I will leave up to the reader. While I can't really comment on the intentions or credibility of the writers and journalists I've cited, I will say that everyone I interviewed while writing this book seemed totally sincere—I wouldn't have included any stories I felt someone was simply making up.

Lastly, I'd like to make it clear that I love Marion, and this book has been a labor of love. Some of these stories are bound to stir up unpleasant memories for some people in town, and for that I apologize. It has never been my intention to hurt anyone with this book. It's true that some of these stories represent Marion's darker side, but I'd like to think that most of us who live here would agree that the good in Marion far outweighs the bad.

Shoe String Jack and the Old City Hall

It was former Marion fire chief Phil Reid who eventually set me straight about the location of the old city hall in Marion. I had sat down with him up at the Marion Public Library to talk about haunted fire stations. Specifically, I wanted to ask him about Fire Station No. 1 (the fire station on South Prospect Street) and whether he had any good stories—preferably ghost stories—to share about the place. Since it's one of the older buildings in town, and since firefighters tend to have a strong sense of tradition, I figured there might be a few good stories to pass along. While Mr. Reid told me a couple of good ones, unfortunately none of them was a ghost story.[1]

However, he did mention something in passing that I had never realized. "You know, there was another fire station before Fire Station No. 1," he said. "It was on the northeast corner of Church and Prospect. Actually, the fire station, city hall and the city jail were all in the same building for years." I did some research and discovered that if I wanted any spook stories concerning a firehouse in Marion, this particular building was the one on which I should concentrate.

Constructed in 1857, the old city hall was never one of Marion's more distinguished-looking buildings. It was thirty-five feet by eighty feet and resembled, if anything, an overgrown one-room schoolhouse. According to the book *History of Marion County, Ohio, and Representative Citizens*, "[T]he lower story [was] used as the Central Station of the Fire Department and as the city prison. The upper part [was] used for the mayor's office, municipal court, police headquarters and sleeping quarters for the firemen." It wasn't

A postcard showing the old Marion City Hall. The location is now a parking lot. *Courtesy of Randy and Sandy Winland.*

a particularly beloved building, either. *History of Marion County, Ohio* goes on to say that "[t]he building will next year be half a century old and is a standing disgrace and eyesore to a city which in all other respects outclasses her sister cities."

On March 31, 1909, an article appeared in the *Marion Daily Star* detailing the story of a one-legged shoestring peddler who committed suicide in one of the cells by, ironically, hanging himself with his shoestrings.

What's more, despite having no knowledge of this suicide, "many of the prisoners who…occupied the cells in the city prison…suffered from the hallucination that the place [was] haunted." However, since most of the prisoners who reported seeing something strange were suffering from delirium tremens (i.e., they were going through severe alcohol withdrawal), police placed little faith in their stories.

Still, a local fireman named Ira Schrock who was at the station at the time of the suicide said that he was convinced that something creepy was going on. In fact, according to the *Star* article, "[H]e was awakened many nights to see the form of the peddler limping through the sleeping apartment of the firemen. So strong did he become in his belief that the man or ghost was really haunting the place that he did not go to bed some nights."

That same year, 1909, another story appeared in the *Marion Daily Star* that also made light of the weird goings-on at the city hall. Whereas the tone of the earlier article had been rather tongue-in-cheek—the witnesses were, after all, the town drunks—this article carries an edge of near hysteria. Rather than paraphrase, I've included the article in its entirety:

Some of the most startling and mysterious things ever heard of in Marion have occurred within the past several days at the headquarters of the police and fire departments. Many people skeptical concerning spooks and ghosts will have to admit that there is something uncanny in the tales that are told of the city hall.

A few weeks ago a fireman resigned his position at the central department because a black snaky object which hovered about his bed at night would not allow him to sleep. The young fireman frequently would jump out of bed in the middle of the night, letting forth the most hideous yell that could come from the mouth of a man. "I see him just as plain. Can you see him standing right there," the lad would ask and the other firemen would sink back in their beds wondering what it really was.

Recently a prisoner escaped from the city prison. The lock on the cell was securely fastened when the officers visited the prison in the morning but the man was gone.

A prisoner confined in a cell a few nights ago swore that he saw the grim face of old "Shoe String Jack" who hanged himself in the prison a few years ago. The prisoner was perfectly sober and claimed that he was not the least bit superstitious. "I could see his face as plainly as though he were living and I could distinctly hear his old crutch pounding on the cement floor," exclaimed the frightened man. He begged of the mayor not to confine him in the terrible place another night, as he said he would be converted into a raving maniac if he were compelled to go through another such experience.

It has been a common thing lately to have prisoners complain of hideous shrieks and groans which they say vibrated through the prison shortly after the midnight hour. There are some men in Marion that would rather visit Hades than be locked one night in the city prison. The skeleton face of "Shoe String Jack" and the tin peddler, both characters having died in the prison, are said to be the most hideous sights imaginable.

Only a few nights ago, the entire fire department was compelled to believe that there is a something that prowls through the corridors at night. It is customary with the police to knock three times on the door leading to the quarters of the firemen when they want the department. The chief…sleeps in a bed near this particular door so that he will be able to hear any signals from the police. On this particular night, there were three thumps on the door. They were given in slow but very distinct order. The chief and several of his fellows jumped out of bed and hurried to the door. It was thrown wide open but it was darkness there and nothing more. The firemen searched the police headquarters thinking that some one had tried to place a practical joke, but there was not a trace of anyone.

The indescribable something has evidently been seen by the fire department horses. Tuesday morning shortly after 1 o'clock, the big gray horse, which is the most quiet docile animal in the barn, almost tore down the stable in its efforts to escape the night prowler. The doors of the stable was [sic] kicked open and the animal was trembling like a leaf when two of the firemen appeared at his side. The horse quieted down immediately after the arrival of the hostlers and remained quiet for the rest of the night.

So horrible and hair raising have been the scenes at the city hall that the head of the police department has found it almost impossible to induce one of the patrolmen to stay at headquarters at night to answer telephone calls. There is but one conclusion. The city halls is [sic] haunted. Not one but forty witnesses will testify to the fact. The ghosts or shade of "Shoe String Jack" has been seen, and it is believed that it still frequents the ancient structure.

By 1911, most of the city offices were scattered around other downtown buildings. Fire Station No. 1 went into service two years later. The actual city hall building was by then already falling into a state of disrepair. And so in 1922, the old city hall—some of its windows missing, its fire bell long gone—was finally razed. Where Shoe String Jack and his fellow ghosts ended up is anyone's guess.

Haunted House or Rumor?

An article that appeared in the *Marion Daily Star* on March 25, 1921, had the titillating headline, "Many People Flock to Haunted House." However, it's probably a better example of how gossip spreads around small towns than it is a legitimate ghost story.

Like so many ghost stories, this one has its roots in a murder that, according to the *Star*, took place at a house located on the southwest corner of Creston Avenue and Niles Street in 1919.[2] This story, appearing in the March 3, 1919 edition of the *Star*, described how Miller Herman, heartsick over having been rejected by Dosha White two years before, showed up at her parent's house and shot both Dosha and her new suitor, Lee "Pat" Patterson. Dosha subsequently died from her injuries, while Lee survived. When Miller turned the gun on himself, it was Mrs. White (Dosha's mother) who, surprisingly, grabbed his hand and diverted the shot so that Miller only succeeded in grazing his scalp. During Herman's trial, Mrs. White testified that she had not wanted him to take his life. She had, in fact, always had the kindest feelings for Herman. She hurried to add, however, that "under the circumstances he should be held accountable."

According to police, Herman, before fleeing the scene, picked Dosha up, kissed her and said, "Goodbye sweetheart. Well, I got you this time." When police found him a short time later, Miller didn't protest his innocence but instead willingly went to jail, where he made a full confession that night. The trial got under way on April 30, and on May 12, 1919, Judge Grant Mouser sentenced Herman to life in prison. When asked if he understood

MILLER HERMAN   MISS DOSHA M. WHITE

The killer and his victim. Herman Miller killed Dosha White on her twenty-second birthday. He was only twenty years old. *Courtesy of the Marion Star.*

the implications of that sentence, Herman replied, "Yes, I know. The only way to get out will be to stop breathing."[3]

Herman's crime, while shocking and senseless, was nonetheless not especially depraved or hard to understand. The man was jealous and angry at having been rejected, so he thought he'd get revenge on his ex and her new boyfriend. Nonetheless, rumors began circulating Marion that the White house was "haunted."

By 1921, the Whites had apparently moved out of the house where Dosha had died, and new tenants, the Henrys, were living there. It was then that haunted house rumors seemed to reach a fever pitch. In March of that year, "hundreds" of people visited the house. The *Mansfield News* reported that "on the night of the second anniversary of [Dosha White's] murder, a pistol shot was plainly heard in the house, but the occupants of the house could not locate the source." The article went on to say that the Henrys often heard footsteps and pounding during the night. They also complained that sometimes the noises were so bad they couldn't sleep.

However, the actual owner of the house remained skeptical. He was quoted as saying, "[I've] never heard of the house being haunted. Other families never complained about it, not even the Whites."

Was the house really haunted? Or were the new tenants simply feeding into rumors about the house, which already had a notorious reputation? The truth, as with so many ghost stories, will probably forever remain a mystery.

MARION'S OLDEST CEMETERY

I f asked to name Marion's oldest cemetery, most people around town would probably guess the Marion Cemetery, home of the famous Merchant Ball.[4] However, Marion's oldest cemetery, dedicated by Eber Baker himself in 1822 when Marion was laid out, is actually situated on a two-and-a-half-acre piece of land on Quarry Street.[5]

Paul and Barbara Midlam did a survey of Marion County cemeteries back in the 1970s and '80s and published the results in their book *Cemetery Inscriptions of Marion County, Ohio*. They wrote that the cemetery has gone by a few different names: the Old Marion Cemetery, Pioneer Cemetery and the Quarry Street Cemetery. As the city's oldest graveyard, it's also the final resting place of a number of historically significant people, including members of Eber Baker's family. The exact number of people now buried there, however, is unclear. Local historian Trella Romine, in a 1983 interview with the *Marion Star*, estimated that up to two hundred people are buried at the site. However, since the records are "scattered about and incomplete," the exact number will probably never be known.

At first glance, the plot of land doesn't look much like a cemetery. In fact, with its trees, the flag in the middle and its frequent use as a playground by neighborhood children, the cemetery almost resembles a park (albeit a boring one). The Midlams offered a few reasons why the graveyard looks so ungraveyardlike. First, the iron fence that once surrounded the property is long gone, and more significantly, many of the tombstones are missing.[6] According to the Midlams, vandals are responsible for the majority of the missing and destroyed tombstones.

Marion founder Eber Baker. His wife, Lydia, died in 1843 and was buried in the Quarry Street Cemetery. However, her remains were later moved to the Marion Cemetery. *Courtesy of the author.*

Various efforts have been made over the years to restore the cemetery, but the success of these restorations has been limited. In a 1989 article about the cemetery appearing in the *Marion Star*, local radio personality Charlie Evers was quoted as saying, "In the 1930s, the local Daughters of the American Revolution (DAR) and others restored the cemetery, erecting and cleaning 168 tombstones. In 1976 the DAR, with the assistance of the Boy Scouts of America, erected a flag pole and set memorial markers next to it for Pvt. David Potts, who served in the Revolutionary War, and his wife."

Today, while no one is seriously discussing restoring the cemetery, there are efforts underway to at least protect it. In an interview with the *Columbus Dispatch*, a member of a group calling itself Friends of Marion County Cemeteries, Diane Walker-Butler, said that she was prompted to take action in protecting the cemetery when she saw cars parked on the land during the Popcorn Festival. So far these protective measures have been modest—the city has since put up "No Parking" signs around the edge of the cemetery—but it's nice to know that some people around town are keeping an eye on the property.

Perhaps the most terrifying bit of history concerning the Quarry Street Cemetery is its role as the final resting place for many of the victims of a cholera epidemic that struck with terrifying swiftness during the summer of 1854.

According to Paul Midlam, this gravestone is not the original but rather dates from 1977. *Courtesy of the author.*

Cholera, a bacterial infection that spreads through contaminated water and causes diarrhea, vomiting and cramps, was a serious public health concern during the nineteenth century. Today, thanks to antibiotics and modern water treatment systems, it has been virtually eliminated in the United States, though it remains a problem in the developing world.

The *Buckeye Eagle*, one of Marion's first newspapers, ran a story on July 20, 1854, marking the appearance of cholera in Marion and calling it the "full scourge of mankind." However, the paper was still relatively optimistic, as there had been, up until then, "but two or three cases, and these amongst the foreign [i.e., non-Marion] population." Unfortunately for the residents of Marion, the epidemic was just beginning.

History of Marion County, Ohio notes that after the epidemic began, "All business was suspended, and the streets were...desolate." According to a book published in 1950, with the long-winded title *Biographies of Many Residents of Marion County, Ohio and Review of the History of Marion County*, "The plague lasted about six weeks, forcing terrorized residents to flee the village and killing sixty-five citizens. The bodies of the victims...are buried in the Old Cemetery."

David Jameson,
Undertaker & Coffin Furnisher,

This ad appeared in the July 13, 1854 edition of the *Buckeye Eagle*. Mr. Jameson would've had his hands full that summer. *Courtesy of the author.*

One of the few remaining upright gravestones in the cemetery. *Courtesy of the author.*

To put that number in perspective, the number of people living in Marion Township in 1850 was 1,311, and the number of people living within the city proper was 980. That means that, at the very least, the epidemic killed 1 out of every 20 people in town and did so within the span of a few weeks. If a similarly deadly epidemic were to strike Marion city today, it would kill more than 2,000 people.

In July 1857, less than a year after the cholera outbreak, a group of Marion businessmen got together to form the Marion Cemetery Association. They purchased forty-seven acres just south of Marion, and Marion Cemetery was dedicated in November 1858.

A new cemetery for Marion was actually long overdue even before the cholera outbreak because the Quarry Street Cemetery was no longer adequately serving the needs of Marion. While it was clearly no longer big enough, the land itself was also not suitable. An article appearing in the *Marion Republican* noted that the cemetery "had become too near the houses of any of our citizen, too near for the purity of the atmosphere, and too near for the purity of our veins of water which fed the neighboring wells, running as they do, over a superficial bed of limestone." The article went on to say that "many of the graves cannot be sunk over 2 feet and a half without blasting the rock, and many are the bodies in that graveyard now, which are not covered with earth over twenty inches, and this within the corporate limits of the village of Marion." The location was also no longer ideal. Charlton Myers mentions that the Quarry Street Cemetery had ceased to be a dignified final resting place for the dead; funerals were often interrupted by passing trains or by rowdy bar patrons from the neighborhood "saloons adjoining the outgrown graveyard."

Another rumor that persists in Marion to this day is that none of the graves in the Quarry Street Cemetery can be opened because the bodies buried there are still contagious. This is actually nonsense. In fact, as the Marion Cemetery began to take shape, many people around town made plans to move members of their family from the Quarry Street Cemetery to the Marion Cemetery—and this was just a few years after the epidemic.

Moving bodies that have been in the ground for a few years, however, is not for the squeamish, and with such a macabre task at hand, rumors began springing up. This article appeared on May 6, 1858, in the *Marion Republican*:

> *Since the process of vacating the old grave yard commenced, many horrible stories have been set afloat in the community in regard to persons being buried alive, as indicated by the positions in which the corpses have been*

found. Every one of those stories, so far as we could ascertain, was without foundation. And whether they were set afloat from malicious motives, or for the purpose of hoaxing others, they have no doubt shocked the feelings of those having friends buried there.

Let the motives be what it may, it is wrong to put such stories in circulation, unless they are absolutely true, for even to raise a SUSPICION in a sensitive mind that a friend had been buried alive, is to drive it to distraction. Let us have no more of them.

With the establishment of the much larger new cemetery, the Quarry Street Cemetery began its long decline, in both importance and upkeep. As Diane Walker-Butler lamented to the *Dispatch*, "People don't even realize what's here, what this is."

THE HARDING HOME

T he entire tour group was just the two of us, which made us feel a little awkward but didn't seem to bother our tour guide. She addressed us as we were a group of thirty people—thirty hard-of-hearing people. "Welcome to the Harding Home," she boomed as we stood on the front porch. "This is where Harding conducted his famous front porch campaign in 1920!"

Although I had grown up in Marion, it was my first tour of the Harding Home. Seth, who had already been on a tour with one of his classes from school, informed me, "It's kind of boring. I mean, you can't even really go into the rooms. Can't take pictures, either."

The tour turned out to be all right, though. Mostly because Seth seemed to know every rumor and scandal that had ever been associated with Harding and his presidency, and believe me, there were plenty. "Is it true that Harding had a black grandparent?" "What about the rumors that he had affairs with other women and one of the women tried to blackmail him?" "I also read that some people believe Florence Harding may have poisoned Harding because she wouldn't allow an autopsy to be performed on him. What do you think?" "Was Harding really a member of the KKK?" To her credit, our tour guide attempted to address all of these questions, though they seemed to fluster her a bit.[7]

Those lurid questions, however, were not the reason we had come to the Harding Home. In researching stories to include on the Spooky Marion website, I had come across the *Haunted Ohio* series by Chris Woodyard, which

The Harding Home. *Courtesy of the author.*

included a couple of fascinating spooky stories about both President Harding and the Harding Home. We had come to see, firsthand, the "Harding Death Clock" and the "Finch of Doom."

THE DEATH CLOCK

According to our tour guide and the *Haunted Ohio IV* book, the clock, which is located on the wall above the first landing of the main staircase, was a wedding gift. For years it worked perfectly, both before and after Harding's death. However, Woodyard wrote that "on August 2, 1973 at 7:30 p.m., the clock inexplicably stopped." This was exactly—down to the very hour—fifty years after Harding's death. Furthermore, Woodyard wrote that "on Thursday, one week later, the clock began to run—as mysteriously as it had stopped on the previous Thursday." When Seth asked our tour guide if the clock had stopped for anyone else since then,

The "death clock" and the "medium's chair." *Courtesy of the Harding Memorial Association.*

she said that Harding Home volunteer (and local Harding High School French and Spanish teacher) Shannon Morris claimed to have seen it stop, though she didn't know when or offer any reasons for why it may have stopped. (For the record, it was ticking away when we saw it.)

THE FINCH OF DOOM

Maybe a more interesting story is the one about a pet once owned by Mrs. Harding. Actually, Mrs. Harding is the central figure in almost every supernatural story surrounding the Hardings and their home. In *Haunted Ohio V*, Woodyard wrote that Mrs. Harding believed in astrology and regularly consulted a clairvoyant named Madame Marcia.

Our tour guide pointed out that the banister posts at the foot of the stairs were carved to look like owls—animals rich in supernatural symbolism—and that a chair in one of the bedrooms with a star and

A postcard showing Warren and Florence Harding relaxing on the front porch of their Mount Vernon Avenue home. *Courtesy of the Marion Public Library Ohio Reading Room Collection.*

moon cut into the back of it was known as the "medium's chair" (though whether a medium actually used it is unclear).

Certainly, however, the oddest story concerned Mrs. Harding's pet finch, Petey. According to our tour guide, Mrs. Harding wasn't particularly fond of the bird, but since he was a gift, she felt obligated to take him. Perhaps to show her displeasure, she named the bird Petey after her ne'er-do-well first husband. Mrs. Harding would cover the birdcage with a cloth at night, and the bird would go silent. However, on the night before Mrs. Harding and her husband were supposed to depart for Alaska, the bird began to sing from beneath his covered cage. For Mrs. Harding, this was a bad omen, and rightly so—Harding died on the trip.

According to Woodyard, Petey ended up outliving both President Harding and Mrs. Harding. Visitors to the Harding Home can now see Petey, stuffed and under a glass jar, in one of the bedrooms of the Harding Home.

THE MARION CEMETERY

THE RECEIVING VAULT

The Harding Home may have been where President Harding spent much of his life; the receiving vault in the Marion Cemetery is where Harding's body was interred in the years following his death. Located near the center of the cemetery, the receiving vault was built to inter the freshly dead until their graves could be prepared. It has also, historically, been the site of some strange activity—activity that, some would argue, continues even now.

Harding began his ill-fated "Voyage of Understanding" in the summer of 1923. The trip was an attempt to reconnect with the American people and restore their faith in his administration, which was becoming increasingly tarnished by scandal. Harding was in Alaska when he became ill with what Harding's personal physician, Dr. Sawyer, initially thought was food poisoning.[8] However, Harding clearly had something more serious than food poisoning, because he died a few days later in San Francisco on August 2, 1923. Today it is generally believed that Harding died of a heart attack. After a ceremony in Washington, D.C., Harding's body was returned to Marion by train, and he was placed in the receiving vault on August 10, 1923. Thereafter, armed soldiers guarded the vault around the clock. On November 21, 1924, Mrs. Harding died, and she,

President Harding being laid to rest in the Marion Cemetery's receiving vault in 1923. *Courtesy of the Library of Congress.*

too, was placed in the receiving vault. There the two of them stayed until December 20, 1927, when they were moved to their final resting place at the Harding Memorial. (The memorial itself wasn't dedicated until June 16, 1931.)

Perhaps at this point it would be useful to explain the purpose of a receiving vault. When people die, they are generally buried within a few days. However, there are situations for which burial may be difficult. For example, a winter burial, especially in the days when gravedigging was done by hand, could be especially difficult, and in that case a receiving vault was a place to inter a body until the ground thawed.

A receiving vault also had to be a secure place because grave robbers (or resurrectionists, as they were known in the nineteenth century) were inclined to steal the body. Fresh corpses were in demand by medical schools, and there were no laws making grave robbing a crime in Ohio. Thus, it is clear why this description of the Marion Cemetery receiving vault, taken from *History of Marion County, Ohio*, includes such detailed information about the vault's invulnerability to grave robbers:

> *The vault proper is provided with solid iron doors, with a fine combination lock, the combination of which is only known to the proper officers of the association.*
>
> *The bodies of the dead placed in the vault are free from danger of the desecrating hands of the resurrectionist, and are safe till they are of no*

further use for dissection, when they are buried. The construction of this vault [renders] *the employment of watchers at graves unnecessary.*

Of course, the guards standing watch over the Hardings were there largely for ceremonial purposes, and it's unlikely that any of them imagined it would be a duty that entailed much action. But then some strange activity—some would argue paranormal activity—began to occur around the receiving vault not long after Harding's body was placed there.

It started with rock throwing. During the years guards were stationed at the receiving vault, there were two small guardhouses flanking either side of it, and while the guards were inside them at night, they could hear rocks striking the houses. Soon after, horns began to sound in more remote parts of the cemetery and at odd hours in the night. When the guards would attempt to track down the rock throwers and trumpet blowers, they were unsuccessful. In any case, the guards weren't too concerned by the mild harassment, which they assumed was the work of mischievous boys. However, as the frequency of the activity increased, the guards began to take the behavior more seriously. Eventually, the guards were granted permission to fire their weapons—M1903 Springfields—into the air in an attempt to scare the perpetrators. That, too, failed to deter the harassment. Finally, the soldiers secured shotguns and buckshot cartridges from Fort Hayes, with orders to "shoot directly at any offenders." Shortly thereafter, the disturbances more or less ceased. When the bodies of President and

The receiving vault in the Marion Cemetery in late 2010. *Courtesy of the author.*

President Harding's funeral procession as it made its way south down State Street toward the Marion Cemetery. *Courtesy of the Marion County Historical Society.*

Mrs. Harding were moved to the present-day mausoleum, the guards followed them over there, and no strange incidents were ever reported from that location. As for the weird activity in the Marion Cemetery around the receiving vault, no offenders were ever caught and no explanation for the harassment was ever determined.

THE GRAVE MARKER WITH THE GLOWING EYES

Let me set the scene: It's about ten o'clock on a summer night in 2008, and my nephew, Seth, and I are walking (trespassing, actually) in the Marion Cemetery, trying to locate one particular grave. Seth is confident that we'll find it, even in the dark. Ahead of us, a vague white shape slowly materializes. It is a woman. "There she is," Seth whispers. "Do you think her eyes will really glow?"

I first heard the story from Joe Howard during a talk he gave on ghost hunting at the Marion Public Library in the summer of 2007. The story goes that the statue of the woman standing atop this particular Marion grave has eyes that glow. Amazingly, the story is true—the eyes really do glow! Seth and I saw it for ourselves. But more on that in a minute.

The story Joe told was actually a story he had heard from one of Marion's veteran police officers. More experienced police officers would prank unsuspecting rookies by driving up to the monument at night and finding an excuse to have the rookie approach the statue. When the unsuspecting rookie would get within a few feet of the statue (which was now brightly illuminated by the patrol car headlights), the officer in the car would suddenly turn off the headlights, leaving the rookie to face a statue with glowing green eyes.

It's a good story and actually pretty funny, but I had my doubts about it. Pranks on rookie cops? Maybe. But a statue with glowing eyes? That's a little tougher to believe. But then Joe said something that changed my mind. "Of course, the car headlights are what make the prank work," he said. "Something—moss maybe—growing on the statue absorbs the light, and by the time the officer in the car shuts off the lights, the eyes are already glowing."

When Seth and I got to the statue, the eyes weren't glowing, of course. But we had brought a huge flashlight. I shined the light on the face and told Seth to shut his eyes so they would stay adjusted to the dark. "Okay," I said, "open them!"

The statue in question. Note the darker spots, especially around the head. These are the spots that glow after being exposed to a strong light. *Courtesy of the author.*

And the eyes were glowing. It was a dull, greenish glow. And while we both knew that there was a scientific explanation for what we were witnessing, it was still unnerving.

While collecting research for this book, I actually tracked down the police officer (who wished to remain anonymous) who was the supposed origin of the story. When I told him what I had heard, he laughed and said that it sounded like I had two stories that had, through retelling, become one. He said that he knows the story about the statue with the glowing eyes, though he had never heard of it being used to prank other cops. He also said it wasn't uncommon, especially in the "old days," for cops to prank rookies, and one of those pranks was for veteran cops to hide in the cemetery before the rookie would drive through and then jump out from behind a tree or building to scare him.

As for Seth and I, we were lucky that we didn't attract the attention of the police (who regularly drive through the cemetery after it closes specifically because of trespassing numbskulls like us). If we had, I suppose we could've explained to the officer that we were trying to get to the bottom of a story about a statue with glowing eyes that we had heard, at least indirectly, from a fellow cop. Somehow, though, I doubt this would've satisfied the officer.

Note: I've been intentionally vague about both the location of this grave and the family name on it. In the original version of this story, which appeared on the Spooky Marion website, I was very specific about these details. However, I later received a letter from the family asking me to remove that information because the statue had been vandalized in the past, and the family was worried that my story might lead to further damage. Of course, I complied.

THE MERCHANT BALL

Although I figure there's only a remote chance of this actually happening, I've already decided that if anyone ever asks me whether there's anything interesting to see in Marion, I'll answer with something along the lines of, "Well, in the Marion Cemetery, there's this massive granite ball that moves on its own and for reasons no one can really explain. Have you heard of it? No? Well, it's pretty famous around town. I mean Robert Ripley himself deemed it interesting enough to include in his "Believe It or Not!" newspaper column in 1929." Hey, it's either that or Buckeye Chuck, right?[9]

For those readers not from Marion, here's the story of the Merchant Ball in a nutshell:

In 1886 the Merchant family of Marion constructed what they thought would be a beautiful and fitting grave monument for their family burial plot in Marion Cemetery. Within two years after its construction, someone noticed that the 5,200 pound polished granite ball atop the pedestal had begun to rotate. The only unpolished spot on the ball was now visible, indicating the ball was on the move. The Merchant family, being concerned about this, brought the erection crew back to the site to re-set the ball. It was not long before the ball again began its now continuous movement.

Various explanations have been proposed for the ball's movement: gravitational effects; the seasonal expansion and contraction of the ball and its base; and seismic activity. Since it's a grave, there are also those who attribute the ball's movement to paranormal forces. However, this

The Merchant Ball in the Marion Cemetery. Note the unpolished spot, evidence that the ball is indeed turning. *Courtesy of the author.*

explanation seems unlikely as well. Christian B. Merchant, the Merchant family patriarch who designed the monument, was a respectable and well-to-do farmer and stock dealer; if there are any strange or creepy stories surrounding him or other members of the Merchant family, they have yet to come to light.

As for myself, I had obviously heard of the Merchant Ball while growing up, but I didn't actually see it until I was an adult and had Seth with me to help locate it. (I had unsuccessfully tried to find the ball once before while alone, but I was only able to find some other huge stone ball that, apparently, doesn't move.) After we finally found it, I stood in front of it scratching my head while Seth snapped a few pictures.

Like so many before who had come to have a look at the Merchant Ball, I had expected to see a bit more, um, action. In their book *Weird Ohio*, Loren Coleman, Andy Henderson and James Willis wrote that soon after cemetery workers noticed the ball's movement in 1904, people began showing up in droves to catch a glimpse of a "wildly spinning two-ton piece of granite." However, in reality the ball moves at a rate of two inches per year.

Still, without a definitive explanation of the ball's movement (scientific or otherwise), it probably remains Marion's best-known mystery.

THE RECEIVING VAULT REVISITED

While reading the *Marion Star* in the early fall of 2010, I ran across an article about a local ghost hunting group called Eerie Paranormal. I ended up dropping them a line just to introduce myself and see if they might be open to giving an interview for my website somewhere down the line. A nice woman named Darcy Hunley almost immediately got back in touch with me and said that, yes, they were more than willing to talk. I called her again in November, and that's when she told me about her group's work at the receiving vault.

At this point, it might be worth it to have a quick look at the history of ghost hunting. After all, groups like Eerie Paranormal have a historical precedent stretching more than 150 years into the past—a precedent that, whether they're aware of it or not, shapes their approach to ghost hunting even today.

What we now call ghost hunting probably has its roots in the spiritualist movement, which really began in the 1850s, grew in popularity for many years and then finally began to lose steam by the 1920s.[10]

Spiritualism, which was never really an organized religion but rather more of a religious movement, promoted the idea that communication with the dead was possible. Communication with the dead took place through mediums, and the sessions in which the living and the dead communicated were known as séances.

One of the factors that made séances so compelling to so many people was that they were great entertainment. As Helen Sword wrote in *Ghostwriting Modernism*, "[G]hosts materialized, voices spoke through levitating trumpets, messages wrote themselves on sealed slates, and mediums' bodies emitted disconcerting quantities of a strange, filmy substance known as ectoplasm." Just as importantly, they offered undeniable "proof" that something supernatural was happening. Of course, for all of the mediums "proving" that they were communicating with ghosts, there were just as many people determined to show that the mediums were simply frauds. Thus a contest of sorts developed in which those who believed in communication with the dead and those who did not sought to demonstrate, using various technologies, the validity of their respective claims.

One of the first technologies used to prove the existence of ghosts was photography. And for a while it looked like photographs offered definitive proof of ghosts, especially after a guy named William H. Mumler produced

A "spirit" photograph taken by S.W. Fallis, supposedly during a séance in 1901. It is actually a double exposure or composite of superimposed cutouts. *Courtesy of Library of Congress.*

a photo of Mary Todd Lincoln with Abraham Lincoln about four years after he died! It was P.T. Barnum, of all people, who thought Mumler was just a con, and he set out to prove so. He hired another photographer to create a photo that showed *Barnum* with Lincoln. (The photo was nothing more than a double exposure using someone who resembled Lincoln.) When Mumler stood trial for fraud in 1869, Barnum produced the photo in court. Although Mumler was actually acquitted of the fraud charges, his career as a spiritual photographer was over, and as Kathleen Zoehfeld put it in her book *Ghost Mysteries: Unraveling the World's Most Mysterious Hauntings*, "Mumler quietly faded into the woodwork."

Today's ghost hunters—whether skeptics or believers—still use cameras. When I talked to Darcy from Eerie Paranormal, she filled me in on the other devices they use: digital video recorders with night-vision capabilities, EMF detectors, digital voice recorders and a laser grid.[11]

When I talked to Darcy in November 2010, she told me that, despite only having formed earlier that year, the organization had already performed six investigations. No bad for a group that began as a group of friends who all had an interest in the paranormal. When I asked her directly if she believed in ghosts, she said that while she considers herself a skeptic, some EVPs and unexplained video images they've recorded have made her more open to the possibility. Still, she said that she's never had any overt experiences with ghosts.[12]

Like me, she had heard stories floating around Marion having to do with the receiving vault in the Marion Cemetery. Hoping to investigate it, they contacted the Marion Cemetery manger, Jim Riedl, to see if he was willing to let them carry out an investigation. They were pleasantly surprised to find that he was both knowledgeable and open to the endeavor.

On Friday, August 20, 2010, Eerie Paranormal began its investigation at about 10:30 p.m. The team consisted of six people, but they initially split into two three-person groups once they got there. Shortly after arriving, group member Bob Lawhun radioed the other group to say that he had just received a slap to the head near the vault by an unseen hand. The other group went over there and set up the cameras.

Not long after the group members were in place around the vault, probably the most significant event of the night happened. Darcy said that she heard some movement behind where she was sitting, but when she turned around, no one was there. This wouldn't have been so noteworthy, but at that exact time, they also recorded an EVP of a male voice saying, "I come home." Meanwhile, Bob Lawhun was at the front of the vault doing an EVP session, and in an effort to get some kind of response, he said, "Maybe if there's a woman in there, maybe you would rather talk with us." This time, the group recorded a female voice responding, "There's no one here." Okay, so it's a ghost with a sense of humor.

I asked Darcy if she could send me the EVP recordings so that I could listen for myself. Honestly, I was pretty skeptical about the recordings, but when I heard them the hair on the back of my neck stood up. The male voice saying, "I come home," is clear. The female voice saying, "There's no one here," is a bit more difficult to make out—it's at the very end—but it's there. But don't take my word for it. These EVP recordings are all available on the group's website (http://www.eerieparanormal.com) under the "Evidence" section.

Darcy said that the group hopes to do another investigation at the receiving vault. Perhaps the next investigation will yield even more EVPs. After all, the simile "as silent as a grave" doesn't seem to apply in this case.

THE HARDING HOTEL

It was a cool fall day when I walked into the Harding Hotel.[13] It wasn't the first time I had been there. My wife had somehow persuaded me to attend a ballroom dancing class with her there in 2007. And although that experience filled me with anxiety—I'm a horrible dancer—at least I had a normal reason for being there. This time was different; *this time* I was going in to ask if the place was haunted.

I was expecting to see a lot of activity when I entered the lobby, but it was utterly quiet. There was a front desk, clearly left over from when it was a hotel, but it didn't appear to get much use. There was also a huge picture of the building's namesake hanging above the piano. More impressive was the large chandelier, which I later learned was another original hotel fixture. I snapped a few photos before wandering up to the mezzanine floor, where a sign said "Office Manager." I figured that was probably a good place to start. However, it was deserted, too. Although the door was open, the lights were on and a radio was playing, no one appeared to be around. Unsure of what to do, I sat down outside the office and decided to wait. After a few minutes, an older woman sporting spiky hair and a bright red T-shirt wandered over.

"Can I help you?" she said.

"Well, I was hoping to talk to someone about the history of the Harding Hotel."

"Uh-huh. Well, Marilyn Skinner is the manager, but she's not here. She'll be back tomorrow. Can I help you?"

"Do you work here, too?"

An artist's rendition of the Harding Hotel published in a pamphlet by the Marion Chamber of Commerce in 1922. *Courtesy of the Marion Public Library Ohio Reading Room Collection.*

"Yes," she said. "I do cleaning and maintenance."

Suddenly, I had an idea. "Well, maybe you can help me."

She looked unsure. "Okay…"

This was the awkward part. I had to explain the premise of this book without sounding like a crackpot. I took a breath and continued. "I'm writing a history book about Marion with an emphasis on local spook stories, hauntings, legends—stories of that sort. Since this is one of Marion's more historical landmarks, I thought I'd drop by and see if anybody had any good stories about the place."

I waited for her to kick me out.

"Well, I've had all kinds of strange experiences in the ten yeas I've worked here. Let's see, one time…" And suddenly she began telling me ghost stories about the Harding Hotel. I could hardly believe it. I pulled out my notebook and tried to keep up.

According to a little pamphlet put out by the Marion Chamber of Commerce in 1922 entitled *Marion, the Progressive City*, Marion had big plans for the

Harding Hotel (which was still under construction at the time). The eight-story hotel was going to be "one of the finest in Ohio" and would make "Marion a stopping point for tourists on the Harding Highway."[14]

When the Harding Hotel did open in 1924, the hotel's namesake, President Warren G. Harding, had already died. Thus, Harding never actually saw the hotel named after him. Nonetheless, the hotel attracted some big names, such as poet Carl Sandburg, humorist Will Rogers and dancer Fred Astaire. When I eventually talked to Marilyn Skinner, she told me that John Dillinger and Al Capone are also rumored to have stayed there, though whether this is really so remains unclear.

The Harding Hotel was also the scene of one of Marion's more spectacular suicides. On November 7, 1963, desk clerk Edith Smock phoned the fire department to say that a man was locked in a room on the sixth floor and that she feared he was gong to jump. As it turned out, the man was the hotel's longtime manager, fifty-seven-year-old Virgil Dye. As the fire department raised a ladder to him and his minister pleaded outside the door for him to reconsider, he jumped to his death.[15]

The old reception desk at the Harding Hotel. *Courtesy of the author.*

Suicides aside, the Harding Hotel was never really the scene of great drama or violence. The hotel continued to operate, gradually losing its grandeur and prominence along with the rest of downtown, until it was finally closed in 1975. For a while there were even plans to tear it down.

Her name was Donna, and she was originally from Sparta, Ohio (a village in Morrow County that makes Marion look like a bustling metropolis in comparison). She said that her duties mainly consisted of cleaning and maintenance. She got about three sentences into her first story when suddenly she said, "Hell, rather than tell you, I'll just show you what I'm talking about."

First we went to the front desk in the lobby. "Bear in mind that I'm usually the first person here in the morning, and I'm telling you that I sometimes hear creaking behind the counter and feel cold spots in the area, even when it's warm. Come over here and tell me if you feel cold." I walked over to where she was, but honestly I didn't really feel a change in temperature.

"Come on, let's go to the basement," she said. "I want to have a smoke anyway." When we got down to the basement, she showed me what used to be a room for dancing and drinking, especially during the Prohibition era. Part of the old bar was even still leaning against the wall. Another room she showed me was full of old pieces left over from when the hotel was renovated back in the '90s: pieces from the cornice molding, ornate iron railing and light fixtures. She tossed me the top of a wooden newel post.[16] "A souvenir if you want," she said. Actually, I didn't really want the hunk of wood, which vaguely resembled a green pineapple, but I took it so as not to seem rude. (It has since grown on me and now sits on one of my shelves, a makeshift bookend.) She eventually led me through to the maintenance room. "This is where I've had a few weird experiences. One morning when I came in here, I turned on the light and suddenly I felt something move up the back of my neck and through my hair. Not like the wind but like, I don't know, a presence." When I asked her how often this has happened, she responded, "All the time."

After Donna finished her smoke, we went up to the third floor, and she told me what was probably her most impressive story. One morning, as she was rounding the corner, she saw a shape hovering in the hallway. She said that it resembled a blue square with pink edges, and the shape appeared to be undulating. She said that she stood there dumbfounded for a minute before the shape abruptly disappeared. She freely admitted that whatever she saw

The third-floor hallways where Donna, my interviewee, claims she once saw something she can't explain. *Courtesy of the author.*

didn't in any way resemble what we tend to picture when we hear the word "ghost." She hurried down the hall to where it had been hovering, which was in front of the AC unit. Although the AC was blowing out cold air—it was the middle of summer—the spot where she had seen it was warm (which is surprising since the sensation of cold is more typically associated with ghosts). In any case, she was quite certain that she had seen *something*, and the experience had left her deeply unsettled. Interestingly, she hasn't seen any strange activity on the third floor since that day.

Before I left, she looked at me and said, "You think I'm crazy, don't you?"

"No," I said. And I was being truthful. I really do think Donna has had some strange experiences at the Harding Hotel, though I'm at a loss to explain them.

Marion came very close to losing the Harding Hotel, but it was eventually saved thanks to the efforts of some dedicated locals who saw the hotel as an important Marion landmark. In 1980, the Harding Hotel was placed on the National Register of Historic Places, and in 1995 the Marion Home and Neighborhood Development organization began renovating the Harding Hotel. The 147-room hotel was eventually transformed into a 67-room apartment building. The renovations ended in the summer of 1997, and a short time later the first residents began moving in.

The Harding Hotel has been one of the success stories in downtown Marion. Hopefully, it will remain standing for years to come, both for the sake of the ghosts that may wander its halls and, more importantly, for the sake of anyone in Marion who appreciates local history.

MRS. WHITTINGHAM SNAPS

Willow Street is a quiet, tree-lined side street just off Presidential Drive near Grant Middle School. Most of the houses are so nicely kept and unassuming that one would probably have a difficult time imagining any of them as the scene of a murder. But that's exactly what happened on a cold evening on February 28, 1973, when Rosemary Whittingham left her home on Mount Vernon Avenue with a .22-caliber revolver and drove to 323 Willow Street to confront Susan Bartee and Susan's husband, Kenneth, with evidence that Susan was continuing to have an affair with Rosemary's husband, David Whittingham. Before the night was over, Mrs. Bartee would be dead and Mrs. Whittingham would be facing first-degree murder charges.

According to the August 30, 1973 edition of the *Marion Star*, David Whittingham came to Marion in 1970 to start a new job with Marion Power Shovel. His wife remained in Moline, Illinois, to sell their house. Alone in Marion, David Whittingham began an affair with Susan Bartee. (How David and Susan met is unclear.) Rosemary Whittingham stated during her murder trial that she noticed a change in David when they did see each other again. Her suspicions were confirmed on Mother's Day 1971, when she confronted her husband, and he admitted to the affair but claimed that it was over.

Rosemary was not convinced, however. According to the *Star* article, her doubts led her to "follow her husband, make note of Mrs. Bartee's movements and phone calls, hire a local private detective and purchase a telephone tapping device." She didn't buy the gun until just a few weeks before the murder. Interestingly, if one believes the defense's argument, Rosemary bought the gun with the intention of using it to take her own life rather than Susan Bartee's.

By early 1973, Rosemary Whittingham had ample evidence, mostly in recorded telephone calls, that the affair between her husband and Susan Bartee was far from over. On February 28, Rosemary went to the Bartee home and, perhaps seeking an ally, attempted to play the taped conversations between David Whittingham and Susan Bartee for Kenneth Bartee. However, Susan, who was also present and none too happy to see Rosemary, insisted that the voice on the tape was a "forgery" and became so loud and disruptive when Rosemary tried to play the tapes for Kenneth that he was unable to hear the taped conversations.

Clearly frustrated, Rosemary prepared to leave the Bartee home. Susan Bartee went to the dining room, leaving Kenneth and Rosemary in the kitchen together. Rosemary asked Kenneth, who was "sitting…with his head in his hands," for a drink of water before going into the other room, where Susan was sitting. Rosemary later claimed in court that she couldn't remember what she did next. However, the evidence was clear: Rosemary shot Susan in the head point-blank. Kenneth, horrified, rushed in and wrestled the gun out of Rosemary's hands before calling the police.

During the trial, Rosemary's lawyer argued that she was temporarily insane during the episode and therefore not culpable for her own actions. However, the prosecution argued that Rosemary, who had a background in theater, was simply acting during her psychological examinations and during her testimony.

On September 1, 1973, after about three hours of deliberation, the jury found Rosemary Whittingham guilty of second-degree murder. On September 14, 1973, Marion County Common Pleas judge Robert Kelly sentenced her to life in prison. The fates of both David Whittingham and Kenneth Bartee is unknown.

This story first appeared on the Spooky Marion website in October 2008, and while it's an interesting true crime story, it's clearly not a ghost story. But then I received an e-mail from a guy named Dean Hileman in October 2010, and his experiences on Willow Street suggest that elements of the supernatural may, in fact, be at play in this story.

Dean moved into his place at 308½ Willow Street in 2008 with Cracker, his Jack Russell terrier. After he moved into his place, he noticed that

Dean Hileman and Cracker. *Courtesy of the author.*

Cracker's behavior changed. In one of his e-mails, he told me that "[i]t all started while sitting in my living room. Cracker used to bark at the wall, though nothing was ever there. [When] I would look outside the window, thinking someone or a squirrel may have been out there, [there was] nothing of significance." Other strange things began to happen to him as well. Since he's lived in his place, he's had the sensation of someone tugging his leg, his TV has changed channels on its own, his electricity has gone off and on for no apparent reason and a female friend of Dean's once felt someone touching the back of her neck despite the fact that no one else was in the apartment.

Dean, believing that something significant and unexplained was happening in his apartment, began to research the house on the Internet. However, while he was unable to find out anything about his place, he did find the article I had written about the house directly across the street. For him, that's when some things started falling into place.

After e-mailing back and forth for a couple of weeks, I finally met Dean face to face in December 2010. When I went over to his place, I was expecting to meet some kind of nut-job. However, that wasn't the case with Dean. In fact, he struck me as both articulate and sincere.

The turning point for him came when he was sitting in his reclining chair and a tube of hair gel that was about three inches from the edge of a table fell to the floor. This was especially unnerving because the tube wasn't even round! Suddenly he had an idea: "I said, 'Susan, if you come into the room, let me know in some way.' That night I heard a pounding…against the wall behind the TV (about four or five times). I thought it may be Cracker in…my living room, but she was asleep in her cage. I lay back down…and the same tapping occurred. I got up again and walked outside thinking my neighbor was making the noise from downstairs, but I found no one home. I told Susan I needed to sleep and the sounds stopped."

As I stood talking to Dean in front of his apartment just before I left, he repeated something he had written in his first e-mail: "I was never much of a believer in this paranormal activity, but I believe more than I used to." Just then, Cracker, who had been fidgeting on Dean's lap, became very still and sat up. I turned to see what had caught her attention, but of course nothing was there. At least nothing *I* could see.

THE PALACE THEATRE

As a kid at Oat Street Elementary School, I remember all of us piling onto busses to go downtown to see *Snow White* or *The Legend of Sleepy Hollow* at the Palace Theatre. Before the show started, someone would inevitably point to one of the statues or a dark corner and claim to have just seen a ghost. The Palace certainly isn't short on atmosphere. Well-known architect John Eberson wanted his theaters, the Palace included, to evoke "an Italian garden, a Persian court, a Spanish patio or a mystic Egyptian temple-yard…where friendly stars twinkled and wisps of cloud drifted." The Palace was designed to make audiences forget that they were in a tough little blue-collar town, and in that regard it succeeds marvelously.

Compared to some of the other buildings in town still standing, the Marion Palace isn't awfully old, but it's been in almost continuous operation since it was opened in 1928.[17] Like the Harding Hotel, the Palace is one of Marion's historic landmarks that saw hard times in the years following World War II. By the mid-1970s, in fact, the Palace was ready to close up for good. At one point there were even plans to tear it down and replace it with, among other things, a gas station. However, a group of concerned Marionites (known at the time as the Palace Guard) was able to raise the funds to buy and renovate the Palace. When renovations began in 1976, the place was in pretty bad shape. Volunteer Jan Augenstein (and my old fourth-grade teacher, and thus one of the people piling onto those busses that took all of us to the Palace) was quoted in the *Columbus Dispatch* as saying that one of the jobs included cleaning floors that had had pop spilled on them since the 1920s. After three

A postcard of the Marion Palace Theatre. Its appearance has remained largely unchanged since it was built in 1928. *Courtesy of the Marion Public Library Ohio Reading Room Collection.*

months of renovations, the Palace was reopened in the summer of 1976 and has remained open for business ever since. But is it haunted? That was, after all, why I was interested in it.

I had originally contacted Palace director Tina Salamone by e-mail to see if she might have some stories about the place or could at least direct me to someone who might. When I talked to her in late 2010, she informed me that she had taken over the job from longtime director Elaine Merchant less than two years before and hadn't heard any stories that fit with the theme of this book. I was almost ready to give up on the Palace altogether, but then my brother reminded me that a kid we had known growing up on Silver Street, a guy named Dan Bradshaw, now worked at the Palace. When I finally tracked him down and laid the premise of the book on him, he told me that while he didn't have any stories himself, he had heard that two different musical directors—Clare Cooke and George Schram—had weird experiences in the Palace.

Although I was unable to track down the elusive Mr. Schram, I did get a hold of Clare Cooke, and she told me enough to make the possibility that the Palace is haunted at least seem plausible. She told me that she generally finds the Palace an eerie place and that she doesn't know any performers

The Palace Theatre stage as seen from the balcony. *Courtesy of the Marion Public Library Ohio Reading Room Collection.*

who enjoy going in there alone. She said that people involved in productions at the Palace often joke about a ghost they've named "Christine."

However, the origin of the Christine story—if there is much here that constitutes a story—is murky at best. As far as actual strange incidences go, Clare did share one particularly unnerving story. She said that once while she was on stage, going through one of her routines, she noticed a light turning on and off. At one point she even left the stage to investigate it. However, the light was in perfect working order, and so she returned to stage. Once she was on stage again, the light once again began to go on and off again. When I asked her about Mr. Schram's experiences, she said that while he was coming into the theater one day, he heard someone warming up when he knew the building was empty.

So is the Palace haunted? I still don't know. What I collected hardly adds up to what one might call a huge body of compelling stories. Nonetheless, as any kid who's been to a show there can attest, the Palace seems like a place that, if it's not haunted, should be!

WITH UNSEEN HANDS

A re there those among us whose senses extend beyond the natural range of perception? So-called mediums or psychics? Or are these people simply charlatans preying on the gullible and simple-minded?

A number of articles appearing in the *Marion Star* in the 1890s specifically addressed the legitimacy of local séances. The articles centered on the Woods residence, a house located on the corner of Fairground and Park Street (though whether this was the southwest corner or the southeast corner is unclear). This was apparently the best place to take part in a séance in Marion at that time.

On February 20, 1893, an article titled "With Unseen Hands" appeared in the paper. The unnamed author writes (rather tongue-in-cheek) that, upon entering the séance room for the first time, he "beheld quite a little multitude of faces unknown to [me] and three gentlemen friends who evidently as skeptics were present to wrestle with spirits."

Mr. Lem McClaid, a medium from Ashley, conducted the séance.[18] On this particular evening, the séance involved a phenomenon called trumpet speaking.[19] McClaid instructed the three women and nine men to form a circle, hold hands and begin singing. "Finally," the *Star* writer noted, "one of the trumpets commenced to circle around the room tapping first this one, then that, and giving [me] an extra whack, evidently recognizing...a rank skeptic." Soon after, voices began to emanate from the trumpet, and for the next two and a half hours, the group listened as the dead spoke to them. Among the departed at this particular séance were an Egyptian who had

This illustration, which originally appeared in the 1921 book *The Life and Mysteries of the Celebrated Dr. Q,* demonstrates what audiences could expect in a so-called trumpet séance. *Courtesy of the author.*

been dead for thirty thousand years, an Irishman ("brogue and all") and, perhaps most surprisingly, a couple of dead locals, including Robert Kerr.[20]

At the end of the séance, the writer wrote that while he remained skeptical, he was willing to admit that he was clueless as to how the trumpets were manipulated. Furthermore, even his three skeptical acquaintances present for the séance were "utterly unable to tell how it was done and glad that they had squandered their lucre in the exploration of the realms of mystery."

Three years later, McClaid still seems to have been in the séance business. However, skeptics were growing bolder in their efforts to prove that the sessions were nothing more than sophisticated trickery. In a *Star* article appearing on January 23, 1896, the author noted that during McClaid's trumpet speaking séance "[o]ne of the skeptics got down on his hands and knees and quietly sneaked across the floor to see who was doing business with the mouth end of the trumpet, but was caught in the act and notice given that another such attempt and the séance would end without refunding the thirty-five cents which McClaid charged at the door to take part in the religious exercises."

Of course, even in the twenty-first century, there has been no shortage of unscrupulous people who are willing and able to convince others of their supposed supernatural abilities. Case in point: according to a *Marion Star* article appearing in 2008, Sherry Stevenson, a Marion woman claiming to be a psychic, allegedly convinced a mentally deficient Colorado man to give her $30,000. In exchange for the money, she had promised him that certain parts of his life would improve. Police later charged Stevenson, who held psychic readings out of her South Main Street home, with fourth-degree felony theft after the Colorado man's concerned relatives contacted them.

The Nelson Street Haunting

A girl I went to school with—I'll call her Lisa—contacted me a while back to say that she grew up in a house haunted by the spirit of a man who had died there. Her story, whether one chooses to believe it or not, has one aspect that's undeniable: the house, located on 770 Nelson Street, does have a very unpleasant history.

He Treated Them Like Dogs

The story really begins on Easter Sunday of 1960. Two girls, eighteen-year-old Virginia Napper and her younger sister, fifteen-year-old Edna Mae, creep up the stairs. Edna Mae has removed her shoes so as to make as little noise as possible. Their mother is cooking Easter dinner, and their father is sleeping in the upstairs bedroom. Ostensibly the girls have gone upstairs to wake their father. Instead, Virginia loads a .22-caliber rifle, slips into her father's bedroom and, with Edna Mae watching, points the muzzle at her father's head. Virginia then pulls the trigger.

At first, police are puzzled by the girls' actions. Both of the girls freely admit to taking part in the killing, but their motive for wanting their father dead isn't clear—at least initially. Marion city police chief Justin Cornely, in a statement to the *Marion Star*, says only that the girls' father had "picked on them." However, it soon becomes clear that Mr. Napper had done more than merely "pick on" his daughters.

Above: Police found Virginia waiting for them here, the .22-caliber rifle loaded and close at hand. She had reloaded the gun that she had used to shoot her father for fear that, even injured, he might still come after her or others in the family. Mr. Napper was, in fact, still alive when police arrived, although he died a short time later. *Courtesy of the* Marion Star.

Below: The Napper family members as they appeared in the 1960 *Marion Star*.

According to Mrs. Napper, the family, which also included two grade school–age boys, was terrified of Mr. Napper. In the words of Mrs. Napper's brother, "He treated my sister and her whole family like dogs." However, it was his two daughters whom he had brutalized the most. In an interview with the *Star*, Mrs. Napper said that her husband had been molesting Virginia for years, and shortly before his death, he had begun molesting Edna Mae as well. Despite the fact that Mr. Napper had threatened to kill the girls if they ever told anyone about the abuse, they eventually confided to their mother what their father was doing to them. It wasn't long thereafter that the girls decided to kill him—a decision their mother seems to have understood. In her interview with the *Star*, Mrs. Napper, sobbing with guilt and anger, declared, "I should have killed him myself—then my girls wouldn't be in this trouble."

THAT GUY IN THE STAIRWAY

For her part, Lisa, who lived in the house until her family moved out in the mid-1980s, says that the family was initially unaware of what had taken place there. It was only after other people told her parents that the family learned about the house's history.

Although Lisa and other family members slept in the bedroom where the shooting had taken place, the ghost seemed to prefer the hallways and stairs, since that's where most of the family members had disquieting experiences. In an e-mail interview, Lisa wrote, "When my sister was younger she would sit and talk to 'that guy in the stairway.' My aunt was scared to death to go anywhere near the upstairs, and she actually wigged out one night and said that there was someone behind her, even though she was the only one upstairs. She ended up breaking her fingernails off in—yes, in—the drywall trying to turn the lights on. My mom saw him in the stairway. She said that it was like he was just staring at her." Lisa herself never saw any ghostly activity directly. However, she did say that "[y]ou always felt like someone was watching or following you."

THE FATE OF THE NAPPER SISTERS

As for the Napper girls, their fates were decided during the summer of 1960. On June 30 of that year, a jury deliberated just over three hours before finding Virginia not guilty by reason of temporary insanity. Although this meant the possibility that the teenager would have to enter the Lima State Hospital for the Criminally Insane, it never actually came to that. On Friday, July 7, 1960, Judge Paul D. Smith found her to be sane and ordered her immediate release. Prosecutor Robert Stout dropped the charges against Edna Mae altogether shortly after Virginia's verdict was announced.

That the Napper girls didn't receive prison sentences for killing their father seems, at least in this particular case, decidedly just, especially considering what they had endured at his hands.

THE MONGOLOID HOUSE

There's a good chance most people who grew up in Marion have heard a Mongoloid House story or two over the years. As a kid in the 1980s, I remember my dad scaring us with stories about a house out in the country where strange people lived (though, for the life of me, I can't remember any of the details). In fact, I would venture to guess that it's Marion best-known local legend.

When I started the Spooky Marion website back in the fall of 2008, the Mongoloid House was at the top of my list of stories I wanted to research. I had originally hoped that there might be some kind of historical mention of the Mongoloid House in one of the books or old newspapers in the Ohio Reading Room of the Marion Public Library. However, I found absolutely nothing. I'm now convinced that the Mongoloid House exists as a purely oral story, passed around from person to person and from generation to generation. With that in mind, I decided that the only way to find out about the Mongoloid House was to talk to people in Marion.

In an effort to get to collect information, I set up a survey in February 2010 on the Spooky Marion website where people could contact me with what they knew. I also talked to friends and family to see what, if any, stories they might pass along.

So far I've heard from more than sixty people, and at this point I've developed some (admittedly flimsy) ideas about the origin of the name; the location in Marion County; and the origin and evolution of the Mongoloid House legend.

Is this house, located on Salem Road, the Mongoloid House? By the time this photo was taken in 2010, a fire had clearly gutted the house. *Courtesy of the author.*

Because it's a local legend, the information I've collected is often vague and full of contradictions and, sometimes, just plain nonsense. Please keep in mind, then, that this chapter is just an attempt to organize that information rather than verify whether it's actually true and correct.

THE HOUSE WITH THE STRANGE NAME

One obvious question about the Mongoloid House concerns the origin of such a strange (and these days politically incorrect) name. Although a few people have said that they know the place as either the Mongoid House or the Salem House, the overwhelming majority of the people I've heard from know the place as the Mongoloid House.

And why, exactly, was it called that? Maybe there really used to be a house out in the county where people lived who were mentally ill or developmentally disabled or just plain weird. Unsure of what exactly made them different, people simply started referring to them as "mongoloids." Survey answers left in response to the question "What stories do you know about the Mongoloid House?" appear to support this. For example, one anonymous contributor wrote:

I've heard various stories, [ranging] from an inbred family to a family with children with mental handicaps. I've heard of people harassing the family with spotlights on the house or other acts of misdeed. I've heard the mongoloid family would throw rocks at cars and hang from the trees or jump out of ditches at passersby or that they would fire shotguns into the air from the house as a warning.

Another person responded with what appears to be firsthand knowledge on the Mongoloid House:

Back in the late 60s and very early 70s, many of us made the trip to the house. Some came out of curiosity and some came to antagonize. The term "mongoloid" was used due to the peculiar looking people living on the property. Were they inbred? Mentally challenged? Who knows? They had high foreheads, big heads, stocky builds and close-set eyes. Some kids would sit in front of the house or in the drive and honk their horns. [The people in the house] would come out and shoot at the cars or beat on them with ball bats. They definitely existed. Can I blame them for shooting and beating on the cars? Not now. When I was young, I thought they were crazy. Now I understand they were responding to the kids who came to antagonize [them]. They eventually moved out of the county. Can't say I blame them.

SALEM ROAD?

When asked about the location of the Mongoloid House, most people said Salem Road just north of Route 529. Indeed, there are a few falling-down buildings on that piece of property. However, there is not much left of the actual house; a fire gutted it a few years ago.

Heather Ingle had this to say about that particular location:

I went to the house in around 1994. The house was standing and walls were all intact. There was graffiti on the walls like "Leave while you can."

The outbuildings located behind the Salem Road house. *Courtesy of the author.*

and *"This is hell." I looked around* [and was] *scared out of my mind. I remember there being a basement but no stairs* [leading down to the basement] *and none* [lying collapsed below] *in the basement.*

Then in 2009 I went back to the house. At the time I didn't know it was the [same] *house. We were just out with friends and* [they] *told us they knew where a haunted house was. So we pull into the driveway, and I told everyone I had been there before. We didn't get out but just took pics. When looking at the pics* [later], *we could see orbs.*

Then in 2010 we went back in the daylight. When we got out, my husband wanted to go to what was left of the house. We looked around and it was super creepy. Each barn was weirder than the next. We took pics to look at later. The creepiest place of all was a tall barn in the back.

However, not everyone agrees about the location of the Mongoloid House. Most of the older (and, in my opinion, more credible) stories come from people who name roads like Kenton-Marseilles Road East, Marseilles Galion Road East and Morral Kirkpatrick Road as the site of the Mongoloid House. For anyone familiar with Marion County roads, these are not even close to Salem Road. What does this information mean? Was there more than one Mongoloid House? Did its location in the local stories somehow change over the years? Many of the people naming roads other than Salem were relating information that was well over thirty years old. Could it be that these people were simply not remembering correctly?

THE ORIGINS AND EVOLUTION OF THE MONGOLOID HOUSE LEGEND

Mongoloid House stories have been circulating around Marion for at least forty-five years. One survey-taker claimed to have first heard of the Mongoloid House in 1964. In addition to the 1960s, every decade that has followed was also represented in both the survey answers and in interviews. Quite a few people even said that they had first heard about the Mongoloid House in 2011. With so many different years represented, it's instructive to examine the evolution of both the stories people have heard and the experiences they have had over the years.

Consider this story related by Debbie Howard about her experience at the Mongoloid House in 1968:

> *There were two families who lived on same side of the road.* [An old man lived in one house while some of his relatives lived in another.] *The home the old man lived in looked like a weathered shack in the weeds. It sure didn't look like anyone could have lived in it. At the time I remember there weren't many other homes on this road. There were two or maybe three other* [houses on the road], *so it was not heavily traveled. If anyone went by the house slowly, stopped or honked the car horn, the old man would come out and chase your car with his car. He had paths through the fields and would use them to cut through and come out in front of your car blocking you. It would scare everyone so much they'd turn around in the road and leave.* [Supposedly] *he had his wife's corpse lying in a casket in his house, but no one really knows. They called the old man "Flash" because of his swiftness. He would come out of nowhere and suddenly be looking right into your car, again scaring those who bothered him and his family.*
>
> *A few of us went out to the Kenton-Marseilles Road location. We drove by real slowly, and before we knew it, headlights were right behind our car*

and gaining on us. Then they were gone. We were laughing when this old
car suddenly came out of the field. We were scared and knew what people
had said about Flash was true, and we didn't stay for more "excitement."

Contrast the previous story with this brief entry from Heather Ayers, who first heard of the Mongoloid House in 2004:

[I've heard] *that* [there are] *hunched back people with big heads that*
are over-sized for their bodies and that they will chase you, then kill you.

Dave Cornelius contributed this story, which he says took place sometime between 1968 and 1970:

While shooting the loop with the car full [of people], *one of the girls*
said, "Let's go out to the crazy people's house."
While sitting in front of his house blowing the horn and all [of us]
turned to the house yelling, an old vehicle suddenly appeared right on the
rear bumper flashing one headlight. Our driver was so busy looking at the
house he waved for the old vehicle to pass. Somebody was getting out of
that old vehicle when I shouted, "He might have a gun!" By then the girls
were crying and screaming as [our] *"slow poke"* [driver] *pulled away*
with the man in pursuit. From then on we called the guy who had chased us
"Flash." And I have never forgotten that night.

Again, contrast Dave's firsthand account with this anonymous contribution from someone who first heard about the Mongoloid House in 2010:

I heard that there was a man who lived there with his sister, and they
had children who were mongoloids, and as soon as he found out, he hung
everyone in the house, set the house on fire and then killed himself.

See the difference? The older stories tend to be much more detailed and personal, while the newer stories tend to be vague and with knowledge that is often secondhand. It appears that the early Mongoloid House stories had their origins in a very specific and real experience (i.e., antagonizing one particular family out in the county), while the newer stories tend to be vague because the family central to the Mongoloid House is, for whatever reasons, gone. In the absence of the "mongoloids," the stories from the last two decades have tended to focus on the Salem Road location. (How this particular property became the focus of Mongoloid House stories remains unclear.) As a result, a location-centered story like the following, told by someone who first heard of the house in 1992, is more typical these days:

> *There were claims that if you drove out on Salem Road, turned off the car and sat there that these people/spirits would come and rock the car and try to get in and the car wouldn't start back up until they left or decided to leave you alone.*

OTHER PECULIARITIES AND LOOSE ENDS

Flash

One character who cropped up in a few of the stories, all of them dating from the 1960s and 1970s, was a guy named "Flash." Since different people mentioned him independently, I can only assume that he was a real person. One person anonymously contributed this experience with Flash:

> *One of my friends drove us out there, [where] we stopped in the middle of the road and waited. In about two minutes, a moderately sized man came from behind one of the buildings screaming like a madman and with a rake. We waited until he could almost reach us and pulled away.*

The real identity of Flash remains unclear. Was he a member of the family that inhabited the Mongoloid House? And what happened to him?

Forgotten Ohio

Long before I put up the Spooky Marion website, Andy Henderson posted a little piece on his website, Forgotten Ohio:

> *The story goes that a Civil War veteran who lived there killed his wife and children and then hung himself in the barn. Today if you visit the barn you might hear the strange noises which many report. The house is also said to be haunted, although it was merely built on the site of the murder house and is not original.*

Andy, who isn't from Marion, told me he that received his information anonymously and has no idea about its origins. In any case, it is very likely that this one paragraph has helped to recast the Mongoloid House story as a haunted house story for a whole new generation of people who have typed "Mongoloid House" (or "Salem House") into an Internet search engine.

As a result, the influence of this story is clear in the Mongoloid House stories of younger people. Kari Hall, who first heard of it in 2010, had this to say:

> The man was a Civil War veteran and he and his wife couldn't have kids. Suddenly she got pregnant and they ended up having 2 kids. During a fight they were having she told him the kids weren't his, and so he killed them in the barn with a shot gun and then killed his wife in the basement before killing himself.

Likewise, Adam Caldwell, who heard about the Mongoloid House in about 2008, offered this variation:

> There was a soldier who lived there with his wife and two kids. He tortured his wife and killed his two kids, followed by hanging himself. The house was burned down, and then built again, but then burnt once again. What I have heard and felt myself is dogs whining loudly and the smell of sulfur in the second story of the barn. If you go into the basement of the house for more than…five minutes, you start to feel things touch you.

The Mongoloid House legend has been around for years, and I suspect that some version of it will be floating around Marion for years to come. Why? For one, people simply love being scared, and the Mongoloid House offers that opportunity to anyone willing to drive a few miles out into the country. More importantly, young people have always been central to the Mongoloid House story, and as long as there are teenagers driving around Marion with nothing to do on a Saturday night, there will always be the Mongoloid House—wherever and whatever it may be.

If you have any stories or information about the Mongoloid House that you'd like to pass along to me, please feel free to contact me at spooks@ spookymarion.com. Photos are also welcome.

TRAINS

I suppose that, like a lot of people in Marion, I have mixed feelings about the trains that rumble through town day and night. There have been times when I've thought I'd lose my mind as a train has rolled slowly by at five miles per hour (or not at all) and made me late for work.[21] Still, who hasn't been lying in bed late at night and listened to the lonesome (though somehow comforting) sound of a train whistle blowing in the distance? Although passenger trains no longer pass through Marion, freight trains—around seventy-five per day according to local train buff David Luyster—continue to pass through town. Quite simply, living in Marion means living with trains.

Although there were two roads passing though Marion in the 1840s, they were not without their disadvantages. For one, the roads were privately financed and thus charged a toll. They were also often impassable in bad weather. Farmers who needed to transport their crops to market needed a better solution, and when the first rail line came to Marion in 1852, the farmers quickly realized the two big advantages trains offered: they were relatively cheap, and they were reliable. As Marion became more industrialized, the importance of the railroads only increased. Clearly, then, trains have always been a fundamental part of Marion's history and identity, and so it should come as no surprise that they turn up in some of the more gruesome and spooky stories as well.

When trying to track down information and stories about trains, my first stop was at the Marion Union Station. For anyone in Marion's who's

A novelty of sorts as an old-timer pulls into Marion Union Station in 1939. *Courtesy of Carol Robinson/Marion County Historical Society.*

never been there, I recommend it. Admission is free (though donations are appreciated), and much like the Harding Hotel or the Palace Theatre, the station is a throwback to an earlier era. The restored interior, complete with benches and ticket counter, make it seem as though a train might arrive at any minute.

The station was first opened in 1902, and in 1907 *History of Marion County* described it as "well lighted, commodious, modern in every respect and a credit to our growing city." The possibilities it represented must have been thrilling, too. Suddenly, somebody from Marion, Ohio, could take a train west to Chicago and Indianapolis, east to New York City or north to Cleveland or Detroit. In fact, Marion was a bustling stop for anyone traveling between those cities. However, train travel didn't last. As cars became cheaper and roads became better, people began to travel less and less by train. By 1971, the year the last passenger train ran through Marion, a clerk at the depot named Robert Krebs estimated that only about fifty people per month in Marion were using the passenger service. By 1986, the station, which had been boarded up for years, was in danger of being torn down. Fortunately, some civic-minded people in Marion bought it and formed the Marion

A postcard showing Marion Union Station in its heyday. *Courtesy of the Marion Public Library Ohio Reading Room Collection.*

Union Station Association. They not only saved the building from being demolished, but they also restored it and turned it into a museum.

On the day I wandered in there, there was a nice older woman at the ticket window. When I explained to her the (by now well-rehearsed) premise of my book, she said that, unfortunately, she didn't know any good stories. She added that many of the men who might have had good stories have passed away. She did, however, point me to a newspaper clipping on the wall that, while not a ghost story, is worth mentioning if only because of how dramatic it was.

In the early hours of February 27, 1949, five rail cars that were part of a New York Central freight train derailed directly in front of Union Station. In purely financial terms, it was a bad accident. However, the accident was made even worse because a young Marion man named Thomas Finch happened to be driving an express truck on the station platform at the moment the train derailed. One of the cars slammed into the platform, causing the roof to collapse on Thomas. Sadly, he left behind a wife and fifteen-month-old daughter.

The unfortunate death of Thomas Finch perhaps illustrates an important aspect of train accidents: they don't happen very often, but when they do, they're often horrific. As a result, train accidents also tend to arouse the morbid curiosity of the public.

This was the case in August 1994 when a local man named Paul Bentley pulled out in front of a 101-car Conrail train at the Kenton Avenue crossing. For reasons that will probably never be known, Mr. Bentley decided to ignore the lowered gates and flashing lights at the crossing and start out over the tracks. Oddly, when he did this he "couldn't have been going more than five miles per hour," in the words of one witness. The train struck the truck he was driving squarely in the middle and dragged it 1,800 feet before finally coming to rest. What adds a macabre element to this story is that the *Marion Star* reported that more than one hundred people (most of them in cars) jammed the area around the accident in order to get a look at the carnage. It was so bad, in fact, that the paper reported that wreckers from R&R Towing had a hard time getting into and out of the accident area. The owner of the wrecking company, Florence Raimo, said that the scene made her sick when she saw the people "hanging around hoping to take a peak at what's left."

While these stories demonstrate the very real danger trains pose in everyday life, trains turn up in a few more ethereal Marion stories as well.

Local historian Carroll Neidhardt published a little book of Central Ohio spook stories in 2007 called *Ghost Stories, Mysteries & Things that Go Bump in the Night*. The book includes the story of Francis Foos, a young man who lived on Likens Chapel Road. The story goes that Francis, having been rejected by a woman, did what any reasonable man would do: he went out and got drunk. While on his way home, he stopped on the tracks at Hoover Crossing.[22] When a train appeared in the distance, rather than move on, he simply waited for it to run him down. His horse survived, and the appearance of this riderless horse is what eventually alerted people that something was wrong. Since then, Neidhardt wrote, "There are nights along those very tracks where some say they see a man yet walking…it is Francis searching for his horse to ride back to his love."

Unfortunately, Neidhardt doesn't make it clear where he heard this story, and I was unable to track down any articles from 1895 that documented either Francis Foos or any railroad crossing deaths. Oddly, I did find a story about a young man named *Clifford* Foos who died in much the same way as Francis Foos, but in 1905 rather than 1895.

Clifford Foos was nineteen years old when he was struck and killed in Centerville by a passenger train, the Chautauqua Express, while out late one night in September 1905.[23] The *Star* reported that Clifford died after he had fallen asleep in his buggy, and his horse had simply stopped on the tracks.

What's especially tragic is that the engineer saw the horse and buggy stopped across the tracks, but he knew that he would never be able to stop the train in time. In fact, rather than slow down, the engineer *increased* speed. He wanted to hit the horse and buggy as hard as possible in order to keep the train from going off the rails—a terrifying proposition for a passenger train. The horse was thrown fifty feet and killed. Clifford's fate was even more grisly. The paper reported that "[t]he whole top of Foos' skull was fractured and his brains were crushed out. His left leg and arm were mashed and the ribs on the left side were broken." After the engineer finally got the train stopped, the trainmen woke the people sleeping in Centerville, and they stood watch over the scene until the coroner arrived later.

Although the article states that Clifford had simply fallen asleep on the tracks, I wonder if that was actually the case. Earlier in the night, Clifford had been out with a female friend, Blanch Northrup, and although they had gone to a roadhouse, she said later that he drank only had a few glasses of beer and wasn't drunk. After dropping Blanch off at her mother's house in Centerville, he turned to go, but not before Blanch told him, "Go straight home. You mustn't go to Green Camp tonight." The article later mentions that Clifford was engaged to a girl from Green Camp, so Blanch's advice not to go there strikes me as rather strange.

Is it possible that Clifford let the train hit him? For starters, if Clifford was engaged, why was he out with another woman that night, and why did she counsel him not to go to Green Camp, presumably to see his fiancée? Was he having problems with his fiancée? Was he also involved with Blanch? Even if he really had fallen asleep, wouldn't the sound of an approaching train have woken him or at least disturbed his horse, especially if he wasn't drunk, as Blanch stated? Of course, this is pure conjecture on my part, but I think the questions are worth considering.

After reading the Francis Foos and Clifford Foos stories, I'm not sure what to think. Either two guys named Foos died ten years apart in startlingly similar ways, or the Francis Foos story is actually a retelling of the Clifford Foos story. The second possibility seems more likely, at least to me. Like so many ghost stories, the Francis Foos story may have its roots in actual events, but the details (the name, the date, the circumstances, the location and more) have changed over time.

Not far from Hoover Crossing—on the same rail line, in fact—there's another railroad crossing that was apparently notorious in Marion County at the end of the nineteenth century. Here is the article as it appeared in the *Marion Daily Star*:

A lonely stretch of railroad tracks crossing Dry Lane Road near LaRue. *Courtesy of the author.*

"Dry Lane" or "Dead Man's Valley" is located near LaRue where a lonely road crosses the Big Four track, and which is looked upon with terror by the superstitious.[24] *It is a wild looking place, and a legend is told of how for years at nightfall a person could be seen standing at the crossing, and when the belated pedestrian or driver would arrive at the crossing the ghostly personage had mysteriously disappeared. A couple of deaths have occurred at this crossing. A resident of Agosta was stealing a ride and fell off a freight train and was killed at this place. Previous to this, a farmer was struck by a train and killed. In this manner the locality gained the named of Dead Man's Valley, but it is more generally known as Dry Lane.*

In years past a number of robberies occurred there, and ever since the road was laid out there has been something mysterious about the place. It is a desolate bit of territory, and when in the autumn, at night fall, the ghost-fearing inhabitants of that portion of the country are passing, they are wont to whip up their horses and cross at a faster sped than their steed is in the habit of traveling.

71

Even now it is looked upon with superstition. The beaux in returning late at night from a call on the belles of the neighborhood will drive a mile out of their way to avoid crossing the lonely spot, and when they do, it is with a mingled feeling of awe and fright, and once across they never look back. Stories of crime and romance are told of the place, but none have ever been proven, with the exception of the robberies long ago.

[It] is one of the romantic localities of Marion County, about which many hair-raising legends are told.

Seth and I decided to drive out to Dry Lane Road to have a look for ourselves. We took 95 West, and just before we got to LaRue, we turned north onto Dry Lane Road. It's still a pretty desolate part of the county, and on the day we were out there the cold, windy weather made it seem all the less hospitable. We parked down the road and walked up to the tracks to get a few photos. As we were finishing up, we spotted a car approaching from the distance. As the driver got closer to us, he slowed down. I figured he was going to ask us if we needed help. After all, we were in the middle of nowhere and on foot. He gave us a long look as he crossed the tracks, but then he abruptly stomped on the gas and disappeared north. Maybe people aren't as helpful as I assumed. Or maybe he knew the crossing well and thought that he was seeing ghosts.

THE MARION COUNTRY CLUB MURDER

A few years ago, while my teenage niece was working at the Marion Country Club, she informed me that there was a ghost that haunted the grounds. While she herself had never seen it, she had heard stories: "I guess there was a girl who got murdered while she worked there by some guy who was obsessed with her. Anyway, now her ghost haunts the golf course."

It's a trivial story—something the teenagers working in the kitchen of the country club probably told one another on slow nights. Whether it even constitutes a ghost story is debatable. It's more like a half-formed rumor of a ghost story. But it's a persistent one, and I've heard it repeated a few times since then. And like so many ghost stories, this one began with a real-life tragedy.

In July 1981, a family canoeing the Olentangy River near Roberts Road discovered the body of a young woman. The body was soon identified to be that of nineteen-year-old Annette Huddle of Harpster. Although no knife or bullet wounds were immediately apparent, Marion County sheriff John Butterworth suspected foul play.

His suspicions were confirmed when, in August 1981, Marion County coroner Robert Gray announced that while it was not exactly clear how Annette had died, it was certainly "violence of an unknown origin."

Unsurprisingly, Annette Huddle's murder was front-page news in Marion. She was, after all, not the kind of girl anyone would expect to find floating in a river. She was young and pretty and, by all accounts, a popular girl. Although she had taken a summer job as a secretary at the Marion Country Club,

The Marion Country Club has long been the setting for ghost stories related to the Annette Huddle murder. However, there is no evidence that this is where the crime actually took place. *Courtesy of the author.*

she had bigger ambitions: she wanted to finish college and become a flight attendant. People in Marion wanted whoever was responsible for her death to be caught. And soon. Unfortunately, that's not the way it worked out. It wouldn't be until 1990 that the killer was finally brought to justice, though for the murder of another young woman and on the other side of the country.

In the course of the sheriff's investigation, one man stood out as a person of interest. Paul Mack was a food and beverage manager at the Marion Country Club and Annette Huddle's boss. Annette had reportedly complained to her family that Mack had sexually harassed her. According to a coworker—the last person to see her alive—shortly before she disappeared she had mentioned that she was going to have "an important meeting [with Mack] about her future."

When the sheriff's office performed a background check of Mack, they discovered that there was a warrant out on Mack for parole violation.[25] They brought him in, hoping to buy time until they could turn up enough evidence against him to charge him with murder. However, that evidence never materialized, and much to their dismay, they had to release Mack. In violation of his parole, he left Marion and headed west, eventually ending up in San Francisco. Marion law enforcement still kept tabs on him through his parole officer, however. In February 1987, a girl named Karen Winslett turned up murdered in San Francisco, and once again Mack was the prime suspect. A warrant was issued for his arrest, but this time he disappeared before police could apprehend him.

On Sunday, March 20, 1988, Mack was featured on the TV show *America's Most Wanted.* An employee at the Marion Country Club—he or she was never identified—happened to see the show that night and recognized Mack. While that was itself not particularly remarkable, the same employee remembered that the country club had received a call from someone in Salt Lake City who was checking the references listed on an employment application belonging to a guy named Sean Paul Lanier. Although the name Lanier was unfamiliar to the country club employee, the dates and job duties fit those of Mack's. The country club employee contacted the Marion Sherriff's Office, which relayed the information to Salt Lake City police, and Mack was captured shortly thereafter.

At the time, Mack was married to a woman—his eighth—by the name of Margie Danielsen. In 2000, she published a book called *Tainted Roses* with the tagline, "I married America's most wanted." Writing about her relationship with Mack, she claims that he was initially "charming, romantic, good-looking and kind." It was only after his arrest for Winslett's murder that she began to learn that he had either lied about or hidden virtually every facet of his life: his arrests, his past wives, his real name and his prison terms.

Honestly, *Tainted Roses* an awful book. Not because it's full of factual inaccuracies but because it's so *boring*. And I'm not the only one with this opinion. The Kirkus Reviews website wrote that Danielsen's writing amounted to "dramatic re-enactments of repetitious moments of inconsequential dialogue involving Mack's blandishments, her fear for her daughters, and her domestic routine. Much of the story reads like a fever dream of undergraduate genre-writing exercises." Still, someone from Marion might find the chapter on Annette Huddle's disappearance interesting if only to read Danielsen's hackneyed descriptions of Marion as a "secluded farming community" full of white picket fences and people who wave to one another. Yeah, Marion's a regular Mayberry.

In any case, Danielsen does a decent job of detailing Mack's trial for the rape and murder of the twenty-one-year-old beauty contest winner Winslett in California. Mack eventually received a sentence of twenty-five years to life for his crime. While Mack was never tried for Huddle's murder, there is little doubt among those involved in her murder investigation that he was responsible. In 2010, Mack was up for parole, but his request was denied, and as of April 2011, he continues to serve out his time at Mule Creek State Prison in Ione, California.

As for Annette Huddle, I don't think she haunts the grounds of the Marion Country Club. It's just a story passed around by kids who could've been her contemporaries if they had worked there in 1981. If Annette Huddle haunts any place, it's the hearts of those who knew her and loved her before she died so tragically.

MARION CAN BE A SCARY PLACE

IN THE BASEMENT

I'm sitting in my friend Bill's pitch-black basement on Halloween wearing an old pair of coveralls and a rubber Michael Myers mask. The whole situation is so singularly weird that I'm starting to creep out myself. But then I hear Bill and his younger brother, Dave, stomp up the front porch steps above. Bill unlocks the front door. He tries the light. "That's weird," he says. "The electric's off."

Of course there's no electric. I had popped out the circuit breaker twenty minutes before, just as Bill and I had arranged. If all went according to plan, we would succeed in playing a killer (pun intended) Halloween prank on Bill's unsuspecting brother.

It was October 2000. I was in grad school and driving to OSU's main campus from Marion. Both the coursework and the commute were totally stressing me out, and hanging out on the weekends with my friend Bill was one of the few things I had to look forward to during that time. Back then Bill was living with Dave on Chicago Avenue, which is just a few streets over from my place.

I've known both of them since I was fifteen or so, and like most brothers, Bill and Dave fight continuously and over the stupidest things, but at the time they had decided to live together because, while neither would admit it, they needed each other. Dave was unemployed and needed a place to live, as well as someone to buy him cigarettes and Dr. Pepper (his main sources of sustenance, far as I could tell). Bill, who is a total slob, needed someone to keep the place picked up and occasionally babysit his daughter while he worked.

One afternoon, Bill and I were hanging out when he mentioned that he had bought a Michael Myers (of the *Halloween* movies fame) mask out at the Southland Mall, and his brother didn't know about it. He did know that his brother was deathly afraid of the Michael Myers character, however. When Bill mentioned this, I told him, "Man, we have to scare your brother with it." And that was the beginning of our plan that would culminate with Dave convinced of his imminent death at the hands of a psychopathic killer.

We decided that while Bill and Dave walked Bill's daughter over to a Halloween party, I would go over to Bill's place, cut the power, put on the Michael Myers costume and wait for them in the basement.

No Rest for the Foreman

Of course, people around Marion have been pulling scary pranks on one another, especially around Halloween, for years. In October 1909, the *Marion Star* ran a story titled "Slumbers of Boss Rudely Disturbed" that describes some road workers attempting to scare their foreman:

> *An old house, said to be haunted, has been the scene of some lively capers near Morral.*
>
> *When H.W. Mann secured the contract for building the Everett Road, he was unable to obtain accommodations at nearby farm houses for his workmen.*[26] *The only thing left for him to do was to provide quarters for his men in the old deserted house, which has been allowed to fall into decay because no family would live in it through fear of ghostly disturbance.*
>
> *"What do we care for ghosts," said the workmen in chorus when Mr. Mann told them that they would have to sleep and eat in the old house. A cook…was speedily secured and the men—about a dozen—took up quarters in the supposed haunted house.*
>
> *The first night everything was peaceful enough—not a ghostly sound being heard.*
>
> *"This house ain't haunted, but we'll haunt her," said one of the workmen to several of the others, "and we'll have some fun with the boss."*
>
> *Old tin cans and kettles were strung up in the attic so that when a rope*

was pulled the din would be terrific. It was arranged that one man should pull the rope the first night and the other fellows should pretend they were frightened. All were "wise" but the boss.

Mr. Mann does not believe in ghosts, but he admits that the boys "had him a-going," and for several nights he slept with his shotgun at his side.

MAN CONFRONTS GHOST WITH "SHOOTING IRON"

Another, even older, account of a ghost-themed prank appeared in the December 17, 1874 edition of the *Marion Independent*. The article was written anonymously and appears to be more or less an attempt to embarrass some local character named Joseph and his sweetie, Myrinda Jane:

Many of your readers will remember that part of the town of Marion once known as "Sloan's orchard."[27] The lot was something less than five acres in size and contained a goodly number of bearing trees of fruit.

At the time it was quite a resort for some young ladies and gentlemen to gather under the trees and talk love and all that sort of thing. A young man, who in that day was as fond of fun as any newly married man ever was of his wife, took it into his head to play "spook" and have his own sport with a "certain" gent and his buxom lass. Knowing the tree under which this fond couple used to unfold their tales of love, he prepared himself with a false-face, a skull cap (as white as snow) and a sheet equally white and repaired one night to the aforementioned tree and perching himself in the highest crotch with the sheet wound around him, he looked, for all the world, like a "sure enough" spook. He had not been there long before this loving pair entered the orchard and so busy were they in "planning for future events" they were seated under the tree without noticing his ghostship. Our ghost listened for some time to their billing and cooing and had well nigh got out of patience when, as the gentleman was about to take one sweet kiss, the lady threw he head back and her face upward, when she sent forth an unearthly shriek! Our Joseph was astonished to hear her "go on so," just because he ventured to do what he had often done before and sought to quiet her. At length after she had run a short distance, as woman only can run, she pointed to "yonder spectre on that apple tree!" "Zounds!" cried Joseph, who stopped long enough to get a fair view of his spookship, and he was just the proper distance from the tree to make the ghost appear to the best advantage.

But our Joseph was a brave boy and Myrinda Jane was a courageous girl (to hear them tell it). Therefore it was agreed that on the following night they would interview Mr. Ghost with a double-barreled shotgun. The next morning the chap who personified the spook took special pains to throw himself in the company of Joseph, that he might the better understand how he had acted his part "up a tree." Joseph was as loquacious as a young crow and let our adventurer into his secret. He was determined to see if that was flesh and blood or a spectre. His old "shooting iron" would tell.

The night for our couple to show their valor came, and shot-gun in hand and Myrinda Jane on Joseph's arm, they wended their way to the orchard. Before they had got within gun-shot range, they beheld the "spirit damned." Joseph knew it would not do to go back on his pluck, and therefore he advanced with a stiff upper lip and his finger on the trigger of his gun until he had got within three rods of the tree. Then taking deliberate aim, bang! *went off the old flintlock, and all the damage the spook received was evinced by a slight rustling of the winding sheet. You may bet all your old boots that Joseph needed someone to help him keep his courage just then and there. Myrinda was not lacking; she told him to fire off the other barrel and take deliberate aim at the beast. Many of your readers will appreciate Joseph's condition when I tell you he had a genuine attack of the "buck fever." But with the encouraging words of Myrinda Jane, and the fact crawling through his carefully soaped locks that if he did not show true grit on this occasion, he would never get her to agree to take him "for better of worse." He then drew a bead on Mr. Spook with a result similar to the first shot. Both now very quietly made their way for the gap in the* [orchard] *fence, but before they got through the fence, they looked back and beheld Mr. Ghost approaching them with a solemn step. It is unnecessary to say there was such a rustling of petticoats and pattering of feet, and Myrinda Jane declared she never made better time in reaching home than on this occasion. At home his ghostship was fully discussed. There could be no doubt about it for* [Joseph] *was near enough to have "knocked the stuffin'" out of a roasted chicken, and yet nothing moved save that terrible winding sheet, which the spook seemed to wave at Joseph as much as to say, "peel away with your old blunderbuss!" The more they talked the more nervous each became so much so that Joseph was almost afraid to go home alone. If it could not be shot with the loads he placed in his trusted fowling piece, they must admit that it was something else than flesh and blood. They voted it a sprit damned. It is proper to remark that the man of the winding sheet and false face had no notions of being shot at; therefore he suspended the articles in the tree in such a manner that he could soon get them down and place them on his person when the shot-gun had been unloaded. He placed himself behind a stump at a convenient distance, where he might have full view of Joseph's performance.*

ALL TRICK, NO TREAT

Scaring one another in good fun is one thing, but sometimes people cross the line from harmless pranks to nasty pranks. During Halloween in 1971, the *Marion Star* reported that razors and pins—*razors and pins!*—had turned up in trick-or-treat handouts. Chief John Long told the *Star* that there had been "four reports of apples implanted with foreign objects—three razor blades and one straight pin." He went on to say that the apples hadn't originated in any particular part of town and that none of the children could recall where they'd gotten the apples. Fortunately, no one was harmed because, in each case, parents had discovered the embedded objects while cutting up the apples before giving them to their kids.

When I first read this story, which was front-page news in Marion, I was shocked. I mean, razors and pins in Halloween candy in Marion? But the more I thought about the story, the more doubtful I became. For one, in the days after the report appeared in the *Star*, no follow-up stories emerged. And every case of tampering was discovered *before* anyone could take a bite? That also strikes me as a bit weird. Most suspiciously, I find it hard to believe that, since the stories emerged from different parts of town, there was more than one person tampering with Halloween treats in 1971.

It turns out that my suspicion is not entirely groundless. In his book *Halloween and Other Festivals of Death and Life*, Bowling Green State University professor Jack Santino wrote that stories of razors and other sharp objects hidden in apples began to spread from the eastern seaboard in 1967. Soon reports of "booby trapped" candy began to appear all over the nation. Interestingly, Santino noted that it was rare for the treats with embedded objects to actually injure kids. Santino also went on to cite a 1985 study by Joel Best and Gerald Horiuchi, who concluded that "virtually all the reports were hoaxes concocted by the children or parents." So while someone was definitely messing with Halloween candy in 1971, I'm inclined to think that attention-seeking trick-or-treaters (or their parents) were just as likely culprits as random sickos.

Sometimes It's Just the Maid

While scaring people sometimes involves a good deal of planning, sometimes we scare each without even meaning to do so.

On March 22, 1922, the *Star* ran a short and humorous article titled "Marion Ghost Proves to be Sick Maid." It relates the story of a young World War I veteran who returned home from work to find his family's house "wrapped in the eerie silence that absence of human occupancy brings in the night hours." A short time later, he began to hear knocking noises coming from somewhere within the house. Although he searched the house high and low, he was still unable to find the source of the knocking. He soon became convinced that the source of the knocking was "not natural" and left to find the rest of his family. Eventually, he located his mother and brother at a neighbor's house, where he told them abut his "ghostly encounter." When the three of them returned to the house, the mother also heard the knocking, but unlike her son, she was able to immediately locate its source. Much to the young man's embarrassment, it was a sick maid who was too weak to call down to the young man when he arrived home.

Out of the Basement

"Come on, guys," I'm thinking as I continue to wait in Bill's basement. "This mask is getting hot."

Bill and Dave are bickering at the door. Bill says, "Listen Dave, I'll go down in the basement and see if the circuit breaker switch needs thrown back on. You wait here."

Dave's not having it, though: "No way! I'm not waiting up here in the dark. I'll go with you, Bill." It's clear from his voice that Dave's already thinking that something is wrong. But then I hear Bill say, "Just wait here. I don't want both of us going down the steps in the dark, tripping over each other."

Bill gets to the bottom of the stairs and pulls out his flashlight. Even though he knows full well I'm down there waiting for him, he still looks momentarily startled when he sees me.

Wordlessly we pull out our props. I have a huge knife made of cardboard and aluminum foil. Bill has a tube of fake blood, which he proceeds to squirt all over himself. Bill then picks up a two-by-four leaning against the wall and starts hitting the stairs and screaming bloody murder. He runs up the stairs, and I hear Dave screaming, "Bill? Bill! What's going on?" By then

The author (left) and his buddy Bill Russell (right) on Halloween of 2000 as they playfully reenact Bill's "murder" for the camera. *Courtesy of the author.*

I'm already on my way up the stairs. I come around the corner and into the living room, where Bill is flopping around on the floor and Dave, in a panic, is still screaming, "Bill?!"

When Dave sees me coming at him in the dim light, he screams, "Oh my God! What the @#%$!?" He backs up and falls over the coffee table and onto the couch, actually has the presence of mind to wing something at me (I later found out it was a pillow—thank God it wasn't an ashtray) and in that moment I actually felt sorry for him. I mean, it was clear he truly thought he was about to die, and the thought crossed my mind that I might actually give him a heart attack. So instead of acting like I was going to stab Dave (our original plan), I leaned down and whispered, "Happy Halloween."

"You @#$%&*!" Dave screamed. Naturally he was really mad at us at first, but after a while even he was laughing about it. To this day, Dave sometimes complains about how mean that prank was, and I have to agree. But even he admits that it was a good one—one of many that have taken place in Marion over the years.

MYSTERIOUS LIGHTS
OVER HINAMON WOODS

Doing research for this book required me to spend a lot of time poring over old newspapers. Old editions of the *Marion Star* are the best (and sometimes only) way to figure out what was happening in Marion at a particular time, and in the course of browsing through old papers, I sometimes happened across weird local stories completely by accident. This is one of those stories.

On September 4, 1905, the *Star*, in an article titled "Ghosts Appear, So Some Think," reported that people in Marion had witnessed strange lights moving in the area of what was known then as Hinamon Woods.[28] In fact, some of the workmen at the Central Ohio Lime & Stone Company even claimed to have been approached by the phosphorescent lights. Take Richard Gillamore, for example. While tending the kilns one night, Richard said that one of glowing shapes floated toward him. Not knowing what else to do, "[he] quoted scripture in a loud and firm voice, and the light winked and went out." Other people in the area were so shaken up that they refused to leave their houses after dark. As for an explanation, the paper could only offer this: "By some the lights are believed to be the spirits of people who have at some time been murdered in the neighborhood. The largest light, however, is credited with being the spirit of a brakeman killed on the Hocking Valley some time ago."[29]

Apparently, the story caught Marion's collective imagination because the *Star* ran a few more stories about the "mysterious lights."

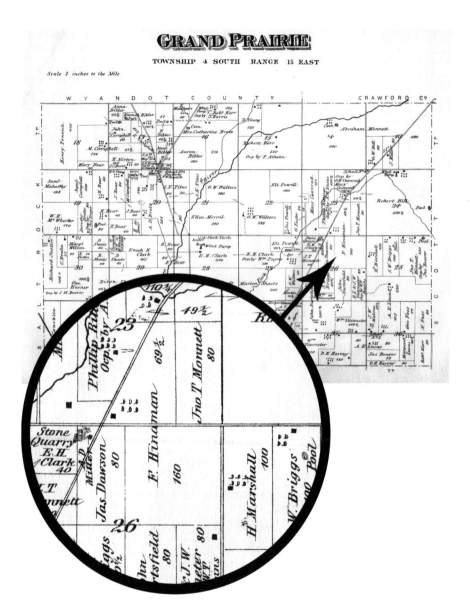

This map of Grand Prairie Township, published in 1878, clearly shows a plot of land marked "F. Hinaman [*sic*]." Was this the scene of the strange activity that occurred in Grand Prairie in 1905? *Courtesy of the author.*

On September 5, hundreds of people in Marion saw a "light [which] appeared some 300 feet from the earth and traveled directly over the Hinamon Woods where it finally disappeared." Witnesses reported that the object had an unearthly color and that the upper portion was covered with red and white stripes. However, to Marion's general disappointment, this particular incident turned out to be a hoax. The "curious light" was, in fact, a balloon sent up by a prankster on Leader Street.

Still, the idea that something strange was going on around Hinamon Woods persisted, hoax or no hoax. On September 6, a group of about twenty young people traveled north of the city to investigate or even capture the "spook." A young woman (who wished to remain anonymous) later telephoned the *Star* and claimed that she and her friends had seen lights in the woods that night at about nine o'clock. According to her, the lights were in plain view for about two minutes before they vanished. They waited a few more hours, but the lights didn't reappear. Although this article, which appeared in the *Star* on September 9, noted that more people were planning trips out to that part of the county, this was the last piece about ghostly lights to appear in the paper.

So what were people seeing around Hinamon Woods? Ghosts? The work of pranksters? UFOs? Some kind of natural phenomena? Or were people just making it all up? Of course we'll never know. But perhaps it doesn't matter. The mystery, after all, is sometimes far more compelling than the explanation.

A True Horror Story

Y ou guys know any haunted houses around Marion?" It was just an idle
question, something to make the time go faster at work. It was July
2008, and I had a summer job as a bike mechanic at Rocky's Cyclery. I had
been telling my coworkers about how my nephew and I were kicking around
the idea of starting a website devoted to Marion's more macabre side.

"I know one," said my coworker Fawn. "My brother lives next to a
supposedly haunted house on Silver Street." Since I'd never heard the story
before, I was immediately interested.

"Yeah," she continued, "it's near the corner of Silver and Commercial.
Supposedly some guy murdered his family there. And there's this thing with
one of the upstairs windows. No matter how many times the owner fixes it,
it always breaks again. That's all I've heard, though."

Little did I know that my one idle question would lead to a story that, by
turns, documents a terribly depressing tragedy but also, if one is so inclined
to believe it, one of Marion's most haunted houses.

I eventually tracked down the story Fawn had mentioned and discovered
that she was basically right. (It turns out that I hadn't heard the story
because I was away at college when it occurred.) As I read through the brutal
sequence of events that had taken place that house, I realized that it was
more than just a local spook story. First and foremost, this was a story of real
evil perpetrated not by ghosts but by the living.

According to the October 11, 1995 edition of the *Marion Star*, Wayne
Thomas, a man with a history of domestic violence, murdered his

The Silver Street house in the winter of 2010. Note the missing windows on the upper floors. *Courtesy of the author.*

girlfriend, Mary Welcome, and her nine-year-old son, Christopher Hook, on Thursday, October 5. Police speculated that "Thomas…beat Welcome's head against the baseboard in the downstairs living room, pinned her to the floor and strangled her. He continued upstairs and cut Christopher's throat with a butcher knife." Thomas himself took the easy way out by shooting himself up with a massive overdose of insulin. Unfortunately, Mary's father, Charles Hook, made the horrific discovery on Saturday, October 7, 1995. He had gone over to the house because he had not heard from his daughter for a few days and had grown worried. Tragically, his concern turned out to be well founded. The three had arrived in Marion only six weeks prior and were renting the house located at 306 Silver Street from Mr. Hook.

I eventually published the above information (in a slightly different form) on the Spooky Marion website in October 2008. I didn't like the story, though. Unlike many of the stories on the website, this one is relatively recent, and that made me uncomfortable. I mean, if this tragic story had happened one hundred years ago, there would obviously be no one around who had known and loved the victims. But with this particular story, it's likely that there are a few people who were familiar with—maybe even related to—Mary and Christopher.

One of those people was Shannon Ward. She contacted me in the early fall of 2010. She had grown up a few houses down from the Hook house, and she shared her personal recollections of Christopher and Mary. Her obvious affection for both of them, as well as her sadness at losing them, lends Christopher and Mary a humanity that the facts I gleaned from old editions of the *Star* cannot:

> *When they first moved in, my brother and I attended the same school as Chris, Oak Street Elementary. We met him at school, and he invited us both to a party his mom was throwing for him. I believe it was a birthday party. We asked our mom, and she said yes and went with us. After that, our moms became good friends. My mom would take Chris to school with us or to the park and vice versa. On the weekends my brother and I weren't staying with our father, we were usually at Chris's house or he was at ours. Mary [was] pregnant at the time, [and she] was due to have a baby in January of 1996.*
>
> *The last day we saw Chris was a rainy Thursday afternoon, when my mom picked all of us up from school. I remember sitting in Chris's room playing with white Play-Doh as my brother and Chris played the Super Nintendo. We were there a few hours when my older sister came to get us for dinner. We asked Mom if Chris could stay the night, but she said no because it was a school night. That was the last time we saw them.*
>
> *The next day, my brother and I stopped at their house to get Chris so we could walk to school. I sat on the porch for a few minutes as my brother knocked on the door over and over again. We didn't hear any movement or noise except for the alarm clock going off upstairs. We figured that they had overslept and we would see them later that day, but Chris never showed up for school and never came back out to play.*
>
> *If Mary had lived, her daughter would be turning fifteen in mid-January, and Chris would be turning twenty-five next year. Even now, they still mean a lot to my family and me.*

As for me, I eventually decided to go down to Marion's west end to have a look at the house for myself. There wasn't much to see—it was just another run-down house in the rough end of town. My old neighborhood. It was a rainy winter day, and windows on the upper floors were indeed missing. The house appeared to be abandoned.

At the time, whether the house was haunted or not was just speculation. Shannon Ward passed along a few of the stories she had heard, though I got the feeling that she felt such stories rather cheapened the memory of Mary and Christopher:

> *I've heard several stories about a red ball that would appear in the upstairs hallway and then bounce down the hall by itself and into Chris's room. There was also a rumor going around about child's laughter in the hallway in the middle of the night. I always refused to go in after the murder. It felt wrong to me somehow.*

Shortly after Shannon got in touch with me, I heard from another woman, Jody Criswell. Like Shannon, she had read about the house on Silver Street, but unlike Shannon she hadn't known anyone involved in the tragedy that had taken place in '95. But Jody and her family had actually lived in the house, and she had her own story to tell.

On a cold winter day in December 2010, I sat waiting for Jody Criswell and Russell Holycross at the McDonalds on North Main Street. Jody had contacted me a few months earlier after she'd read about the Silver Street house on the Spooky Marion website. She said that she had lived there from June 2008 to June 2010 and that she had some stories about the house that I might be interested in hearing. When I asked her if she would be willing to sit for an interview, she agreed. Although she and Russell aren't married, they told me they've been together for more than twenty years and have numerous children and grandchildren between them. The following is a condensed version of the interview I conducted with them, and I will make it the last word on the Silver Street house:

> *Josh: You lived there long after the murders took place. Were you familiar with the story before you moved in?*
>
> *Jody: No. The first day we were moving some stuff in, we took a break and were sitting on the porch. A few people from the neighborhood stopped by and said things like, "You're really moving in there? Do you know what happened?" And then they would tell us what had happened. They said the longest that anyone had lasted had been four months. I wish somebody had told us that before we moved in there.*

Josh: You rented the place, right? Did the rental company ever mention what had occurred there before you moved in?

Jody: No, they never said a word about it.

Josh: How long were you living there before you noticed anything strange?

Jody: The first couple of months were quiet. But, of course, that changed.

Josh: During the time you lived there, did any of the strange activity seem to occur more often in certain parts of the house?

Jody: The bedroom upstairs. We replaced the glass in that window three different times, and every time it shattered. Even now there's no glass in that particular window. They were always blown inward. A lot of weird things happened in the basement, too. And there was one particular incident in the attic.

Josh: Well, let's get into some of the strange incidents that happened at the house.

Jody: One story I think I brought up in an e-mail was about my collection of angels. I had a collection of over two hundred of them. Well, one time me and my two daughters were sitting downstairs, and we heard this crash. One of the girls had this full-size mirror, and we thought it had fallen over. We went upstairs and looked in their rooms, but there wasn't anything wrong, and then we went and looked in my bedroom, and my angels were all in the middle of the floor all broken up. They somehow went from the wall to the middle of the floor.

Josh: How many kids do you have?

Jody: We have nine children between us, but only the two daughters lived with us there. The others are all grown. They were fifteen and sixteen when we moved in there.

Josh: Who slept in the room that had belonged to Christopher Hook?

Jody: My youngest daughter, Sarah.

Josh: Did she have any strange experiences?

Jody: Sarah kept telling me she kept hearing voices. And bear in mind we didn't know any of the people involved [in the murder]. *Sarah came to me one morning and said, "That little boy's name is Christopher, mom." And I said, "What little boy?" "Christopher. He came to me and said he wanted to play." "What little boy are you talking about?" It was only later that we found out there was a boy who had lived there who was named Christopher. One night, Sarah was asleep upstairs, and we heard this commotion, and me and my other daughter, Tiffany, went upstairs to look, and the mattress appeared to floating above the bedsprings, and Sarah was asleep on top of it. We got so scared we both ran back downstairs. The next day she told us she had had some weird experiences in the night, and we were like, "We know; we saw it." Something else odd was that if we didn't leave the TV on cartoons upstairs, destructive incidents would occur. Like the dishes would fall out of the cupboard. But if we put cartoons on, it would all calm down.*

Josh: Did one of the sisters seem to be more affected?

Jody: Sarah. Definitely Sarah. Sometimes she'd go to take a bath, and when she'd come out she'd have scratch marks all over her legs. Even now she has scars from that. Even for a time after we moved out, she kept having these crying spells. When I asked her what was wrong, she said, "Christopher didn't want me to leave." And I just wondered what I was going to do if it continued. She's normally a sweet girl, but while we lived there, she got really hateful, but after we moved out, she became her old self again.

Josh: What about the other sister, Tiffany?

Jody: Now Tiffany would always see a man figure, and every time she saw him, something would happen. Something dramatic. One night she saw him, and she got really scared and just kept saying, "Something bad is gonna happen, something bad." Well, we finally got her calmed down and in bed when my oldest daughter came pounding on the door saying her dad got put through a window. Tiffany suffered from insomnia while we lived there and withdrew and wouldn't leave the house if she didn't have to.

Josh: Were either of you ever alone at the house much?

Jody: Yeah, sure. I didn't really have much happen to me. It seemed like everything centered on the girls. Sarah was especially afraid because she thought that if she talked about it, something would follow her.

Josh: Since you've moved down to George Street, nothing weird has happened?

Jody: No, nothing. The two girls have always been close, but while we lived on Silver, they couldn't get along—couldn't even look at each other—but as soon as we moved out, they were okay again.

Josh: Did anyone else—anybody visiting, for example—ever have any experiences while over there?

Jody: My one-year-old granddaughter, for example. She came over one night one time, and while we were cleaning up my bedroom, we heard what sounded like little bouncy balls going down the steps, and she just froze and said, "Grandma what was that?" When we went to look, there really were three little balls at the bottom of the stairs. We have no idea where the balls came from.

My grandson, if he had to go to the toilet, he'd never go upstairs by himself. "Something's up there grandma," he said. When Russell's oldest daughter, whenever she'd come over, dishes would come flying out of the cupboard at her, and she was like, "I'm not going into the kitchen."

My oldest son also refused to stay there. He spent one night there and later told me that he would never stay there again. He was twenty-seven at the time. He was a grown man and wouldn't stay there. My nephew came to stay with us for a while, and he said, "I'll take the basement." He spent one night down there, and the next day he said he couldn't stay there anymore. "I don't wanna talk about it. I'm outta here." My father came over to visit one time, and he said, "I'll never come back to this house. There are bad things in this house." And he never came back to visit again the whole time I lived there.

Now he visits me more than he ever did in the two years I lived on Silver Street. And I live in a second-floor apartment. Then my mom would come by; she wouldn't even come in. She'd just pull up out front and honk her horn, and I'd have to come out and talk to her.

We had an old guy who worked up at Red Cab as a dispatcher, and he came and stayed with us for, oh, three months. And he was a total skeptic.

Anyway, he stayed in the basement, and one day he said out of the blue, "I'm moving out." And when I asked him why he said, "I saw a man standing over me with a knife, and when I went to reach for him, he wasn't there. I am out of here." And before that he had been like, "You guys are crazy." When he left, he took his clothes and sent other people back to collect the rest of his stuff.

Josh: Did you ever mention any of this to you landlord?

Jody: He just said, "I know there was a murder there, but I don't believe any of that stuff."

Josh: Do any other strange experiences come to mind?

Jody: The house had an attic, which was off of my bedroom, and sometimes we'd hear what sounded like somebody up there walking around. Well, one night me and my two daughters and a friend of Tiffany's [were at the house]. They were like, "Just go up the steps with your phone, stick it in the room and take a photo." It came out as a white shape.

Josh: You wouldn't still happen to have the photos, would you?

Jody: No, that phone turned up missing.

Russell: You could never keep that place warm. Even in the summer, it was always cold in there. I also had a picture of Jesus that I got from my dad that we had hung at the bottom the stairs that wouldn't stay on the wall no matter what I did.

Josh: Do you consider yourselves religious?

Jody: Oh yeah. I believe there's higher power.

Josh: Did you ever look to religion to deal with what you were experiencing in that house? I mean, did you ever pray, for example?

Jody: Yeah, we thought about getting somebody to come in, but Sarah was afraid that somebody coming in would just make things worse, so we never went through with it. I remember somebody told us to get a Ouija board, and I thought, "No way." That would be asking for trouble.

Josh: Did you have any pets at the time?

Jody: We had our dog, and sometimes we'd put her down in the basement if people were coming over. And the whole time she was down there, she'd cry and cry and cry, and when she finally came up, her hair would be standing on end and her eyes would be red. She's never growled or anything—a real easy-tempered dog—but she hated that basement.

Josh: You said that the neighbors kind of warned you before you moved in. Did you talk to them while all of these strange happenings were going on?

Jody: When we lived there, one of our neighbors asked us if we had a small child who cries, and I said no. These were people who had moved in about three months before we moved out. "Well when we're on the side of the house we hear what sounds like a little boy crying." I told her I only had the two teenage daughters.

Josh: These were people on the west side of the house?

Jody: Yeah.

Josh (to Russell): What did your buddy across the street say?

Russell: He told me that we were either idiots or brave as hell because nobody who lived there before us had lived there for more than four months. And he had been living [in the neighborhood] *for about fifteen years.*

Jody: And I had a friend who lived down on Silver Street. She told me, "You guys must be good people because you've lasted the longest there." And when people would move out, it always seemed sudden and usually took place in the middle of the night. There were times when the girls would say, "Come on mom, let's just go. Let's get out of here, now." And then they'd change their minds, like, "No, let's just stay." Especially Sarah. It was like something was keeping her there. Just as quickly she wouldn't want to move.

Josh: When the time came, did the weird stuff going on contribute to your decision to move?

Jody: It was definitely part of the reason. On the last day we were there, our oldest grandson, who is fifteen, was there. We'd just gotten the last of the stuff out. It was me and him and Tiffany in there. And Tiffany said in the empty house, "If there has been something here all along, give us a sign." And suddenly we heard the sound of somebody walking across the floor upstairs. And our grandson was gone. He was out the door and told us he was never coming back in that place.

Russell: "Grandpa, I'm coming to work with you!" is what he told me.

Josh: So it wasn't that the rent was too high or that you had problems with your neighbors?

Jody: No, we got along with the neighbors and the rent was $400 a month, which was reasonable for a full house.

Josh: How did the move go?

Jody: When we decided we were moving, it was like, "Okay we have to get started," but we had a really hard time getting going. And we've moved numerous times. We packed up a box of books one night, and the next day they were all unpacked again and back on the shelf. It was like whatever was in that house didn't want us to leave.

Josh: Before you moved in there, did you consider yourself…did you believe in the supernatural?

Jody: Before living there, I'd never had any experiences like this. This definitely made a believer out of me.

HEADLESS HADDIE

I imagine that if I asked someone who grew up in Marion if he or she had ever heard of Headless Haddie, the response would most likely be some head scratching followed by a "No." If I asked a former Boy Scout of a certain age, however, that guy might get misty-eyed for a moment before replying, "Oh yeah. At Camp Owens back in '65." Headless Haddie, you see, terrified young Scouts for the seventy-odd years she haunted the grounds of the Camp Owens Boy Scout camp out in Pleasant Township.

Most people not involved in the Boy Scouts—myself included—are not really familiar with Camp Owens. The Owens family began letting the Scouts use part of their land for camp-outs back in 1925. As a show of gratitude, the Scouts named the camp after the Owens family patriarch, John A. Owens. In 1967, Clifford and Mabel Owens officially signed the deed over to the Scouts. However, by this time the Scouts had largely outgrown the camp. Camp Owens was about 55 acres, and national Scouting standards suggest at least 1 useable acre of land per boy. By the mid-1960s, there were well over one hundred boys using the camp at the same time. That part of Marion County was also becoming more crowded with housing developments, and the peace and quiet that was a necessary part of the camping experience was becoming harder to maintain. That same summer, 1967, the executive board of the Heart of Ohio Council began making plans to purchase more than 240 acres of land in Morrow County. This would eventually become Camp Wyandot, the Heart of Ohio Council's main campground today. Nonetheless, the Scouts continued

The weed-obscured entrance to Camp Owens is still visible from Owens Road. *Courtesy of Seth Hunt.*

to use Camp Owens for primitive camp-outs until 1995. Since then, the property has generally remained unused, though the entrance and a weed-choked sign are still visible from Owens Road.

I came across the Headless Haddie story purely by accident. While I was an undergraduate majoring in English at OSU, I worked in the OSU Folklore Archives. This sounds impressive, but it was actually just a musty basement room in Denney Hall packed full of filing cabinets. Every quarter, OSU students who take one of the English Department's folklore classes have to do a final paper, and the majority of the students donate them to the Folklore Archives. As a work-study student, my job was to enter the information of thousands of projects that have accumulated down there into a database. One of database fields I had to fill in when entering the information was the county where the student had gathered his or her information. With the idea for searching for projects from Marion County in mind, I decided to make another trip to the Folklore Archives at the main campus. The archivist, a grad student named Cassie, informed me that the

Folklore Archives are currently located in Ohio Stadium.[30] When I got there, I could see right away that the archive was an even bigger mess than when I had worked there. Despite heroic efforts by Cassie, we were only able to locate two files having to do with Marion County. One of them, dated 1975, was on Headless Haddie.

The kid who worked on the Headless Haddie paper—he'd be in his fifties now—was named Mike Sankey, and he interviewed the members of two different troops, most of them in their late teens.

This story, collected from a nineteen-year-old Scout, was typical:

> *I learned about* [Headless Haddie] *when I was a Boy Scout out at Camp Owens, which is south of Marion. The story goes* [that] *there's a farm…which is a little bit north of the camp, and a couple lived there, and the wife's name was Haddie. And one day the neighbors stopped by because they hadn't heard from either Haddie or her husband for a few days, so they stopped by and they found her body but no head. The head had been chopped off. And the husband was never found. And so she haunts the camp and the area around there.*
>
> *There's a small quarry at the edge of the camp, and it's way off away from* [the rest of the camping area]. *Now* [the quarry's] *just a swampy boggy area. And people say that's where she's been seen.*

All of the Headless Haddie stories that Sankey collected share a few common characteristics. Namely, Haddie occupied a farmhouse located near the camp, and someone—either her deranged husband or bloodthirsty thieves—chopped off Haddie's head, and she now haunts the camp looking for it.[31]

Of course, these stories were used mainly to scare younger Scouts. As one of the interviewees tells it, "All the tenderfoot Boy Scouts were always told to be in early and never to [go] out late at night, especially to go to the latrine, for fear that Headless Haddie might come along and…chop their heads off."

To further prove the authenticity of their stories, the older Scouts would often show the younger ones the remains of the old farmhouse that stood just north of the camp. As one interviewee put it, "[R]umor has it that you're usually pretty safe unless you go back and touch the foundation [of the house]. And we always tell the Scouts [the story] after we've taken them back to walk around on the foundation, so it makes them even more scared."

Hoping to get a little more information about Headless Haddie, I made my way over to the Heart of Ohio Council's Marion Scout office to see

Three Scouts enjoying themselves at Camp Owens in July 1933. *Courtesy of the Marion County Historical Society.*

if anyone there had heard anything about Headless Haddie. It turns out that not only had they heard of her, but they also had a book that offers an explanation about the origins of the story. It is perhaps even more interesting than the actual ghost stories.

The book, *Yours in Scouting*, is put out by the Heart of Ohio Council and offers a wealth of information about the history of Scouting in Central Ohio. However, it was the preface to chapter 11 that caught my attention:

> *Every Scout past his first campfire knew about the abandoned house near camp. Although barely visible through the overgrowth which swallowed its walls, this history was the subject to annual exaggeration. And despite warnings, no Scout could resist the chance to see for himself.*
>
> *The home had once been part of a prosperous old German colony that spread through Pleasant Township during the 19th century. The young master of the house bought a life-size plaster statue of a beautiful young maiden as a gift for his new wife. She placed it in her front garden where it stood as a decoration for many years. When spring rains and harsh winters began to take their toll, she moved her lady to an upper porch for protection. The precautions did not help—the likeness of the young maiden eroded and eventually the head tumbled to the ground below.*
>
> *The legend was born one moonlit night when neighbors riding by looked through the pines at the darkened house and saw the glowing form of a headless maiden standing at the upper window.*

Although the authors of *Yours in Scouting* do not say where this story comes from, it certainly seems plausible as an origin story for Headless Haddie.

One snowy afternoon, I decided to drive out to Camp Owens to have a look at the property for myself. It's actually located right next to the Pleasant Township Park, and that's where I parked. The lot was empty that day. After a short hike, I made it to the actual camp property. There were "No Trespassing" signs clearly posted every twenty or thirty yards, but I ignored them. The snow on the property was undisturbed; clearly I was the first person to wander back this way in at least a couple of days. After walking a few hundred yards, I began to see decrepit buildings—the remains of the camp. But then an odd thing happened: I got spooked, though not because I was afraid of being pursued by Headless Haddie. Rather, I could only think about how embarrassing it would be if a neighbor or—God forbid—a sheriff's deputy showed up asking me what I was doing. And so I hightailed it back to my truck, leaving Camp Owens and Headless Haddie—or what's left of them—in peace.

THE DOWNTOWN YMCA

By the time the Church Street YMCA closed its doors in 2004, stories that it was haunted had been circulating for years around Marion. The majority of these stories seemed to focus on the third floor, where the jogging track was located in the final couple of decades of the Y's operation. Like most ghost stories, they were always vague and went something like this: "Hey, I heard that sometimes you can hear footsteps on the track when nobody's there."

What a lot of people don't realize is that this particular rumor probably has its roots in an actual tragedy that took place on the third floor of the Y in 1974.

The YMCA on Church Street was built in 1953 to replace the original, which was located just around the corner on South State Street. (You didn't know that the YMCA on Barks Road is actually Marion's third one, did you?) Today most people around Marion tend to think of the Y as primarily a place to work out. However, affordable sleeping rooms were also once a common feature of many YMCAs, and the Church Street YMCA was no exception. The sleeping rooms were, in fact, located on the third floor.

On August 21, 1974, a cleaning woman found twenty-year-old Ronald McDaniel dead in his room on the third floor of the Y. The Marion County coroner said that he had died of multiple stab wounds some time during the night. By all accounts, McDaniel was a quiet, hardworking young man who was well liked by everyone, and his murder both horrified and outraged Marion. Because some of his belongings were missing, police

The original YMCA, located on South State Street, was opened in 1893 and served Marion until the new downtown Y was opened in 1953. *Courtesy of the Marion County Historical Society.*

soon suspected that Ronald's murder was simply a robbery that had gone horribly wrong.

On August 30, police charged a thirty-year-old Toledo man who was also renting a room on the third floor of the Y—a guy named Terry Lee Lampkin—with McDaniel's murder. Ironically, Lampkin had already been arrested hours after the murder on an unrelated charge. In Lampkin's car, police found a knife they believed to be the murder weapon, and a woman who had dated Lampkin testified that he had stopped by her place and dropped off a small television, a tape player and a toolbox, all of which had belonged to Ronald McDaniel.

In what the *Marion Star* called a "stunning reversal," Lampkin suddenly decided to plead guilty to the murder of Ronald McDaniel on January 14, 1975, just before the second day of his trial was about to get underway. In

The downtown YMCA in 2010. *Courtesy of the author.*

the months leading up to trial, he had maintained his innocence. Lampkin's lawyers refused to comment on why their client had suddenly changed his mind. Perhaps he felt guilty. Or perhaps he realized he stood very little chance of winning his case in the face of such overwhelming evidence against him. In any case, Judge Robert Kelly promptly sentenced Lampkin to fifteen years to life, and that was the end of the trial.

Is the tragic murder of Ronald McDaniel the origin of the Church Street YMCA's supposed third-floor ghost? It would certainly make sense.

In March 2011, I once again talked to Darcy Hunley of the local ghost hunting group Eerie Paranormal. I had interviewed her in November 2010 about an investigation that her group had carried out at the receiving vault at the Marion Cemetery, and a few months later she dropped me a line to say that her group would be conducting an investigation of the downtown YMCA in February. When I talked to her a few weeks after the team wrapped up its investigation, she filled me in on what they had found.

It turns out that a local company, Quality Masonry, owns the building. After Darcy called there and left a message explaining who she was and what her group did, a man named Jeff Johnson called her back. Jeff is more or less the caretaker of the building, and Darcy said that he was surprisingly open to the idea. It turns out that he's had a few experiences in the building himself, and he was hoping that Eerie Paranormal could "prove I'm not crazy."

The hallway on the third floor of the downtown YMCA, where sleeping rooms were formerly located. This is also where the paranormal investigation team Eerie Paranormal experienced unusual activity. *Courtesy of Darcy Hunley/Eerie Paranormal.*

So on a cold February night, Eerie Paranormal—Hollie Beard, Bob Lawhun, Terri Meade, Darcy Hunley, Ben Meade, Rusty Beard and Gary Hunley—settled in at the Y. Before leaving them, Jeff Johnson did a walk-through to make sure that the building was empty.[32] He also turned up the boiler for them.[33]

For obvious reasons, they focused their efforts on the third-floor track, and this is where they collected all of the evidence they later posted on their website. Before they carried out their investigation, Jeff Johnson had told them about his experience with the third floor. While standing outside of the building one time, Jeff looked up to the third-floor windows facing Church Street, and he saw a man standing there wearing a white T-shirt—despite the fact that he knew no one was in the building. As it turns out, Darcy also collected evidence from the Church Street side of the track. She told me that shortly after setting up for the night, she took some photos of what appeared to be an empty track. However, when she examined them after the investigation, she said that the shape of a man is visible in a couple of them. In addition to the photos, they also captured voices on tape. Although I would assume that any voices captured on the third floor would be male—in the 1974 murder, both the assailant and victim were men—the voices appear to be a mixture of both men and women.[34]

In addition to the third floor, the group also decided to check out the basement. Jeff Johnson had suggested that they make this part of their investigation because he's had a few experiences that he couldn't easily explain (e.g. doors slamming when they shouldn't). Although the group did indeed have one uncanny experience in the basement—Darcy said that when she and teammate Terri opened the door to the basement, they clearly heard movement in the dark—they were unable to document any significant activity down there.

After their investigation, Darcy told me that she had gone over the evidence with the current owners, and they thought that the material Eerie

Paranormal had collected was compelling enough to warrant a follow-up investigation. Of course, if the building sells, they might not get the chance. But if the sale of the old YMCA means the building would once again be put to good use, even Marion's local ghost hunters might approve.

ODDS AND ENDS

In the course of doing research for this book, I occasionally came across old newspaper articles that fit with the overall theme of the book but were not substantial enough to warrant an entire chapter. Unsure of what to do with these pieces, I stuffed them in a folder I had labeled "Odds and Ends."

Then, in December 2010, I was talking to Marion Historical Society director Gale Martin when she mentioned that local historian Keith Kohler might be worth contacting because "[h]e has a whole collection of weird stories relating to Marion's history." After a few phone calls, I stopped by his place one night, and he did indeed hand me a whole stack of interesting tidbits he had culled from old local newspapers and magazines. With my "Odds and Ends" folder significantly fuller, I've decided to include some of them after all.

Be warned, however. These articles raise a lot of questions but offer very little in the way of explanations.

A Haunting in Prospect Township

The following article, titled "Spooks and Witches," appeared on April 23, 1857, in the *Marion County Republican*:

> *We hear of an interesting case occurring in Prospect Township. A. rented a house from B. and refused to pay for it, whereupon B. sued for his money*

and, on the trial, testimony was given by A. going to show that the house was haunted. It was a jury trial and instead of B. getting the pay for his house, the jury rendered a verdict of 15 dollars damage in favor of A. So much for owning haunted houses for other people to live in! We thought the days of hobgoblins, spooks and ghosts were over with; but we were mistaken as this verdict, rendered by four gentlemen of Prospect, proves.

THE GHOST CAR

This weird article, "'Ghost' Car Reported Seen Near Prospect," appeared in what I'm assuming was the *Marion Star*. Unfortunately, both the article's source as well as its date are missing:

A ghost car, much like the one reported on U.S. Route 40 in Clark County, was reported seen around midnight Friday on Route 23 on Newman's Bridge south of Marion.

A man driving a car…reported seeing [an oncoming car] *turn off its lights, and the whole car glowed in the dark.*

After the car passed, its lights went on again and drove on. Deputy Sheriff Elmer Ullom said he has not been able to confirm the report, but hopes to continue the investigation. He said he doesn't know if it is the same car reported on Route 40.

THE MAN IN THE WINDOW

This creepy article, "Man at the Window," appeared in the *Marion Star* on August 10, 1897:

Residents of Big Island Township are much concerned over the strange specter that can be seen by day and night from the road in front of the farm of Dr. Bowdish. It is said that a man, well dressed, wearing a black coat, white shirt, black necktie, dark haired and with one arm partially hiding his face, can be seen looking out of the window toward the road at all hours.

Strangers in passing the house have noticed this, but thought nothing of it. Residents of the neighborhood were affected differently, however, and have several times examined into the presence of the strange person, but upon approaching the house nothing was to be seen. The vision seems to disappear into space when anyone approaches the house.

There is a family residing in the property, but they do not seem to be affected in the least by this strange optical illusion. The one topic of conversation in the neighborhood, however, is of this strange apparition.

Christopher Gracely, who lives near the Bowdish farm, often heard his neighbors talking about the strange appearance of the man at the window and his equally strange disappearance, [and he] decided to look into the affair. He passed the house and sure enough the man was seen peering at him from the window, with his arm partially hiding his face as if to shade the light from his eyes.

Sunday Mr. And Mrs. William Manz were guests of friends in Big Island Township. The first thing they heard was this remarkable story. Mr. Manz laughed at the matter, and his friends became indignant that he should doubt their statements. They invited him to investigate. He did so, and found it just as they described. He did not go up to the house, but stopped in the road and looked long and earnestly at the figure, shadow, ghost or devil or whatever it may be.

"FOR RENT $10 WITH GHOST: $8 WITHOUT GHOST"

This article, appearing in the *Marion Daily Star* on June 15, 1910, carried the provocative headline "The Parkers Vacate the Haunted House":

Less than two weeks ago C.H. Parker, an employee of the Marion Steam Shovel Company, laughed heartily when he rented a house from Louis Goldberg through the real estate agency Bryan & Stoll for eight dollars a month with the stipulation that there would be no spooks prowling about.

"I am not afraid of ghosts," declared Parker who had read the sign tacked to the house: "For Rent—$10 with Ghost; $8 without Ghost."

Parker wanted a house in the neighborhood, the Goldberg dwelling being located on Scranton Avenue, and he immediately rented it with the minus-ghost provision because it was cheaper to do so.

But Parker did not count on his wife's fears. He moved into the house with his family June 1st. The Parkers had occupied the dwelling only a few days when mysterious noises were heard. Mrs. Parker became so nervous that she almost suffered an attack of hysteria. She imagined that she saw an apparition of a woman at night, and the result was that the Parkers moved to a house on Davids Street Tuesday. The supposed haunted house is now vacant.[35]

THE GRAVE IN THE ROAD

This last item concerns a grave that stands out in Marion County by virtue of its unusual location—the edge of Cardington Road!

Every Sunday from February 1960 to February 1961, a local lawyer by the name of Charlton Myers broadcast a fifteen-minute segment on WMRN. The subject matter was generally local history, and the transcripts of those broadcasts were eventually collected in a work called *Tales from the Sage of*

John Grimm's final resting place, located on Cardington Road. *Courtesy of the author.*

Salt Rock. In the book Mr. Myers provided some of the back story about the grave in the road.

Mr. Myers wrote that the grave is the final resting place of a man named John Grimm. Apparently Grimm was struck by a falling tree at that exact spot in 1833. For reasons unknown, that is where his wife decided that he should be buried. The grave is easy to spot while driving along Cardington Road—it's surrounded by four upright concrete slabs that surround the original (and now nearly illegible) gravestone.

Perhaps because of its unusual location, John Grimm's grave remains relatively well tended—certainly more than the graves located in the Quarry Street Cemetery—despite the fact that it's nearly two hundred years old.

Notes from the Author

Shoe String Jack and the Old City Hall

1. Mr. Reid told me that there's a cistern located inside Fire Station No. 1. Some of the firefighters would occasionally prank rookies by propping up a fishing pole with the line leading into the water. They would then hand the guy the pole and tell him to holler if he got any "bites." Unbeknownst to the rookie, the other firefighters had also rigged the end of the line so that they could tug on it, thus provoking the soon-to-be-embarrassed fireman to holler, "I've got one!"

Haunted House or Rumor?

2. I drove down to Creston and Niles, and Creston (which runs east–west) meets Niles (which runs north–south) in a "T." There's only a northeast corner and a southeast corner. Either the *Star* was wrong in reporting the location of the house or Creston went farther west in the 1920s.
3. By chance I ran across Herman's obituary in the *Marion Star*—he died in 1953—but it only said that he had died in Columbus, where "he had lived many years." Whether those many years were in the state penitentiary is unclear. He is buried in the Marion Cemetery.

MARION'S OLDEST CEMETERY

4. See "The Marion Cemetery" chapter.
5. Not to split hairs, but Quarry Street Cemetery is Marion's first clearly documented cemetery. There was an even earlier cemetery, though its location is disputed. Local historian Carroll Neidhardt claimed in a 1983 interview with the *Marion Star* that it was located where the present-day water tower stands. Charlton Myers, in his 1960 WMRN radio show, claimed that it was located on South State Street near Columbia Street.
6. An interesting but unsubstantiated story around town is that the city removed many of the upright tombstones to make mowing the land easier. Supposedly, many of the stones are now buried beneath the hill in Lincoln Park, though why they should be there is anyone's guess.

THE HARDING HOME

7. Believe it or not, these questions are not as half-baked as they sound. As recently as April 2008, the *New York Times Magazine* ran an article about Harding titled "Our First Black President?" that examined the rumors that followed Harding's family history. What's more, the *Washington Post* ran an article in the late 1990s about an affair Harding had with Florence Harding's friend, Carrie Phillips. After threatening to go public with the love letters Harding had written to her, Phillips was able to successfully blackmail him for large sums of money. Gaston Means, in his 1930 bestseller *The Strange Death of President Harding*, suggested that Florence Harding murdered her husband. Of course, Means, a lifelong con man who died in prison, was not the most credible or meticulous writer. But rumors that Florence Harding killed her husband persist to this day. Finally, in their 2005 national bestseller *Freakonomics*, Steven Levitt and Stephen Dubner wrote, "By the 1920s, a revived Klan claimed eight million members, including president Warren G. Harding, who reportedly took his Klan oath in the Green Room of the White House." However, one of Levitt and Dubner's main sources for their information about Harding came from Stetson Kennedy's autobiography, *The Klan Unmasked*. They later had some serious questions about the veracity of the claims Kennedy made in that book and said as much in a 2006 article that appeared, again, in the *New York Times Magazine*.

The Marion Cemetery

8. Dr. Sawyer left his own mark on Marion history. Today he is famous for misdiagnosing the cause of Harding's death (he claimed that Harding had died of a stroke) and even hastening, through the use of purgatives, Harding's death. (Actually, many people would argue that Sawyer, who had studied homeopathic medicine, was ill-qualified to treat a common cold much less a serious ailment like a heart attack or stroke.) Dr. Sawyer also let his mark on Marion's landscape. The ramshackle apartment building on the corner of South Main and West Pleasant Street was originally constructed as a sanatorium for the treatment of Sawyer's patients. He later opened the White Oaks Sanatorium in 1908, which eventually became Sawyer-Ludwig Park.

9. For those readers who had the misfortune of not growing in Marion, Buckeye Chuck is the city's celebrity groundhog. According to the Ohio Historical Society, Chuck has been predicting the arrival of spring since the 1970s. The Ohio Legislature made Buckeye Chuck the state's official groundhog in 1979.

10. To read about Marion's own spiritualist connection, see the chapter "With Unseen Hands."

11. Ghost hunters argue that ghosts actually generate their own electromagnetic fields. Thus, when they pick up these fields in a location where they shouldn't exist (e.g., a graveyard), this indicates the possible presence of a ghost. Of all ghost-hunting equipment, the laser grid is probably the coolest. As anyone who's ever taken a high school physics class or, better yet, been to a seedy campus dance club knows, a laser's beam becomes visible if it passes through a reflective substance like smoke. A laser grid projects a pattern of dots on the walls, and the idea is that if a ghost passes through the room, it will cause either a disruption in the pattern on the wall or make the laser beams themselves visible.

12. EVP stands for "electronic voice phenomenon." Basically, one leaves some kind of audio recorder running while asking questions. The idea is that a sensitive recording device can capture sounds and words that human ears might not hear. It's then possible to listen back to the recordings later to see if there's anything on the tape. Critics of EVPs contend that they consist of nothing more than background noise or stray radio transmissions that are interpreted by listeners as language.

The Harding Hotel

13. For the sake of clarity, I will refer to the building as the Harding Hotel, though it's officially been the Harding Centre since it was reopened in 1997.
14. Harding Highway is more commonly known as Route 309.
15. The reason for his suicide was never made public, and while I'm sure that there were people around town who knew why he did it, I was unable to track that bit of information down.
16. A newel post is the post at the top or bottom of a flight of stairs, and it supports the handrail.

The Palace Theatre

17. Believe it or not, Marion's oldest building that's still in use is located at 127–131 South Main Street, where Baires Deli, Dented Dings & Things and D&J's Vibrant Colors are currently located. It was built in the 1830s, nearly one hundred years before the Palace.

With Unseen Hands

18. Ashley, which is a village a few miles east of Waldo in Delaware County, continues to be a home of sorts to spiritualists in the area. Margaret Fling founded the White Lily Chapel in her home in 1949 after she claimed that the spirit of a Native American girl named White Lily began speaking through her. The church has since relocated to a bigger building in Ashley and now employs "5 ordained ministers and 8 working mediums [who] participate in the Sunday and Wednesday services by delivering lectures, conducting healing meditations, laying on of hands, spirit portraits and spirit messages."
19. In his 1908 book *Physical Phenomena of Spiritualism: Fraudulent and Genuine*, Hereward Carrington explains "trumpet speaking" as follows: "There are mediums known as 'trumpet mediums,' whose specialty is the production of voices, etc. thorough a trumpet, these voices often being recognized by sitters as characteristic of their departed friends, as giving information previously unknown to them, etc. In the vast majority of cases, the trumpet talking is done by the medium himself. If the séance is in the dark, the medium's task is an easy one, he having only to wave the trumpet about and imitate whatever voices he desires. By attaching a trumpet to the end of the telescopic rod…

and moving this about, voices can be made to appear in various parts of the room at will. Sometimes the trumpet is partly in sight, when the room is only partially darkened, and yet the voices come. This is accomplished by a small piece of rubber tubing being attached to the mouth of the horn, and the medium speaks into the other end of this tube. The voice appears to issue from the horn. At other times the medium employs a second trumpet, speaking into that, and it is almost impossible to distinguish the difference by locating the sound. At other times the medium consents to be held by two sitters while the horn is doing the talking. When this is the case, the medium generally has a confederate who manipulates the horn, does the talking, etc." Incidentally, not all of the séances conducted at the Woods residence involved trumpet speaking. An article appearing in the *Star* on March 6, 1896, describes how two mediums from Cleveland, Mr. and Mrs. Lindy, conducted a "light" séance (i.e., they kept the lights on during the séance). For this particular séance, Mr. Lindy allowed audience members to tie his hands together and then sew the sleeves of his jacket to his trousers. He was then seated behind a curtain with only his head protruding through a hole. The article noted that "[d]uring the evening cut flowers were passed out from behind the curtain by hands that could be seen, bells were seen to come up from behind one of the curtains and touch him on the head, and then the audience threw their handkerchiefs into the medium and they were passed out [folded]." The journalist's only response to this manifestation of the spiritual world was a backhanded compliment: "The deception was clever."

20. According to *History of Marion County, Ohio*, "Robert Kerr...was one of the most prominent citizens of Marion County as well as one of the wealthiest men and largest land-owners. Mr. Kerr was a man of public spirit and enterprise and was prominently identified with many of the improvements of Marion and Marion County."

TRAINS

21. As anyone who's ever worked at Whirlpool knows, there's no excuse for being late that's more worthless to a supervisor than "But I got caught by a train!"

22. Hoover Crossing is probably located between LaRue and New Bloomington where DeCliff Road and Agosta LaRue Road meet. This seems to be a likely location since Hoover Crossing Cemetery is located there.

23. Centerville is an unincorporated community in Pleasant Township lying roughly three miles southwest (as the crow flies) of Green Camp. On aerial maps, the abandoned passenger line that ran from Green Camp to Richwood is still clearly visible, and it cuts directly through Centerville.
24. The Big Four was also known as the Cleveland, Cincinnati, Chicago and St. Louis Railway. It was formed by a consolidation of four midwestern regional railroads serving the principal cities of Cleveland, Columbus, Cincinnati, Chicago, Indianapolis, Detroit and St. Louis.

The Marion Country Club Murder

25. Mack had managed a somewhat notorious bar in Bucyrus called the Mad Bull. He was on parole after embezzling money from BOS Corporation, owner of the Mad Bull. Incidentally, the bar burned down in an arson fire in 1987.

Marion Can Be a Scary Place

26. "Everett Road" does not appear on the current map of Marion County, and my attempts to find out where it may have been located were unsuccessful.
27. Unfortunately, the location of "Sloan's Orchard" has also been lost.

Mysterious Lights Over Hinamon Woods

28. The location of Hinamon woods remains a bit unclear. However, I think I've located it. While looking at the *Atlas of Marion County, Ohio*, I was able to locate a property marked with the (apparently misspelled) name "Hinaman" just north of Marion in Grand Prairie Township. If you take Route 4 north, between Marseilles-Galion Road East and Moral Kirkpatrick Road East on the right side, even today there is still a sizable woods at that location.
29. In addition to being responsible for braking the train, the brakeman also made sure that the train cars were properly coupled and that the axles didn't overheat. He also checked the train cars for stowaways and shifting cargo. At the time, it was a hard and often dangerous job, and brakeman deaths were not uncommon.

Headless Haddie

30. A lot of people don't realize that there are a huge number of offices and facilities located within Ohio Stadium. In fact, there was a dorm for students with limited financial means located on the western side of the stadium for more than sixty years. I should know—I lived there from 1995 to 1997. Sadly, because of the renovations that took place in 2000, the stadium dorm is no more.

31. In a few versions of the story, the teller says that Haddie was actually the wife of John Owens. However, in these versions of the story, it is always thieves and not Owens—the camp's namesake—who do the chopping.

The Downtown YMCA

32. Jeff explained that walk-throughs were necessary because animals and occasionally homeless people (!) get into the Y.

33. Darcy told me that they nearly froze that night anyway. It's debatable whether this was more the result of paranormal activity (ghost sighting are often associated with temperature drops) or simply the inadequacy of an old heating system in the middle of an Ohio winter.

34. They also spoke to a few current employees at the new Y who had also worked at the downtown Y, and they informed Darcy of two drownings, one in the women's health center and one in the swimming pool. That would explain the female voice they recorded. This is all anecdotal, however. Neither Darcy nor I have been able to find any evidence in the newspaper about any drownings, though I suppose it's possible.

Odds and Ends

35. This story, at least to me, makes even less sense than the others. Why, for example, was the house more expensive with a ghost? Shouldn't a haunted house be less expensive? And for that matter, how could Mr. Goldberg assure the presence of a ghost?

BIBLIOGRAPHY

SHOE STRING JACK AND THE OLD CITY HALL

Looking Back: Historic Images of Marion County, Ohio. Vancouver, WA: Pediment Publishing, 2003.

Marion Daily Star. "Cells and Corridors." March 31, 1909.

———. "'Haunts' at the City Hall." 1909.

Marion Star. "Chief McFarland Preparing to Retire, Recalls Fire Fighters' Rough Tactics 50 Years Ago." December 13, 1943.

Romine, Trella H. *Marion County 1979 History.* Marion, OH: Marion County Historical Society, 1979.

HAUNTED HOUSE OR RUMOR?

Mansfield News. "'Haunted' House." March 25, 1921.

Marion Daily Star. "Herman Sane, Witness Says." April 30, 1919.

———. "Many People Flock to 'Haunted House.'" March 25, 1921.

———. "Sentenced to Pen for Life, Herman Unmoved." May 12, 1919.

Marion Star. "Miller Herman." July 30, 1953.

Marion's Oldest Cemetery

Buckeye Eagle. "Cholera." July 20, 1854.

Census.gov. Census of Population and Housing, 1850 Census. http://www.census.gov/prod/www/abs/decennial/1850.html.

Gibson, Bob. "Old Cemetery Slowly Fading Away." *Marion Star*, March 27, 1983.

The History of Marion County, Ohio. Chicago, IL: Leggett, Conaway & Co., 1883.

Jarvis, John. "Only Vandals Seem to Notice…." *Marion Star*, February 26, 1989.

Marion Cemetery Association. "History." http://www.marionohiocemetery.com/History.htm.

Marion Republican. "Dedication of Marion Cemetery." November 11, 1858.

———. "Wrong." May 6, 1858.

Midlam, Paul J., and Barbara Midlam. *Cemetery Inscriptions of Marion County, Ohio.* Marion, OH: Marion Area Genealogy Society, 1984.

Myers, Charlton. *Tales from the Sage of Salt Rock of Marion County, Ohio.* Marion, OH: Audsam Printing Co., 1996.

Wainfor, Steve. "Marion Group Wants to Help Forgotten Cemeteries." NBC News. November 5, 2010. http://www2.nbc4i.com/news/2010/nov/05/marion-group-wants-help-forgotten-cemeteries-ar-282038.

Wilson, Ruth E., and Sylvia D. Wilson, eds. *Biographies of Many Residents of Marion County, Ohio and Review of the History of Marion County.* Galion, Ohio, 1950.

Zachariah, Holly. "Repairing History at Marion's Quarry Street Cemetery." *Columbus Dispatch*, November 14, 2010.

The Harding Home

Anthony, Carl Sferrazza. "A President of the Peephole." *Washington Post*, June 7, 1998. http://www.washingtonpost.com/wp-srv/style/features/harding.htm.

Gage, Beverly. "Our First Black President?" *New York Times Magazine*, April 6, 2008. http://www.nytimes.com/2008/04/06/magazine/06wwln-essay-t.html.

Levitt, Steven D., and Stephen J. Dubner. *Freakonomics.* New York: William Morrow, 2005.

———. "Hoodwinked?" *New York Times Magazine*, January 8, 2006. http://www.nytimes.com/2006/01/08/magazine/08wwln_freakonomics.html.

Means, Gaston. *The Strange Death of President Harding.* New York: Guild Publishing Corporation, 1930.

Woodyard, Chris. *Haunted Ohio IV: Restless Spirits*. Beavercreek, OH: Kestrel Publications, 1997.

———. *Haunted Ohio V: 200 Years of Ghosts*. Dayton, OH: Kestrel Publications, 2003.

THE MARION CEMETERY

BBC. "History of Modern Spiritualism," http://www.bbc.co.uk/religion/religions/spiritualism/history/history.shtml.

Columbus Dispatch. "Ohio Groundhog Buckeye Chuck Predicts Early Spring." February 2, 2011. http://www.dispatch.com/live/content/local_news/stories/2011/02/02/02-buckeye-chuck.html.

Donegan, Brenda J. "Receiving Vault that Held Harding Need Repairs Again." *Marion Star*, December 14, 2008, 5A.

Dunn, Charles W. *The Scarlet Thread of Scandal: Morality and the American Presidency*. Lanham, MD: Rowman & Littlefield Publishing Group, 2000.

Ferrell, Robert H. *The Strange Deaths of President Harding*. Columbia: University of Missouri Press, 1996.

The History of Marion County, Ohio. Chicago, IL: Leggett, Conaway & Co., 1883.

Koblentz, Stuart J. *Marion*. Charleston, SC: Arcadia Publishing, 2004.

Marion Cemetery Association. "Merchant Family Memorial." http://www.marionohiocemetery.com/Historical%20Sites.htm.

Marion Daily Star. "Guard Duty at Vault Is Serious Business." January 2, 1924.

Marion Star. "Bodies Moved from Vault to Memorial." December 20, 1927.

Ohio Historical Society. "Buckeye Chuck." http://www.ohiohistorycentral.org/entry.php?rec=2399.

Payne, Phillip. *Dead Last: The Public Memory of Warren G. Harding's Scandalous Legacy*. Athens: Ohio University Press, 2009.

Portsmouth Daily Times. "Disturbance at Tomb of President Harding." January 3, 1924.

Russell, Francis. *The Shadow of Blooming Grove: Warren G. Harding in His Times*. New York: McGraw-Hill, 1968.

Schertzer, Bill. "Harding Vault Donor, History Revealed." *Marion Star*, December 14, 2008.

Slatzer, Robert F. "The Monument that Moves!" *Beautiful Ohio* 2, no. 3 (1960).

Sword, Helen. *Ghostwriting Modernism*. Ithaca, NY: Cornell University Press, 2002.

Willis, James A., Andrew Henderson and Loren Coleman. *Weird Ohio.* New York: Sterling Publishing, 2005.

Zoehfeld, Kathleen Weidner. *Ghost Mysteries: Unraveling the World's Most Mysterious Hauntings.* New York: Aladdin, 2009.

THE HARDING HOTEL

Donegan, Brenda J. "There's a Harding Party Planned." *Marion Star,* September 16, 2007.

Marion Chamber of Commerce. *Marion, the Progressive City.* Marion, Ohio, 1922.

Marion Star. "Virgil F. Dye Killed in Fall." November 7, 1963.

McGee, Adrienne. "Grandeur Returns to Marion Landmark." *Columbus Dispatch,* August 26, 1997.

MRS. WHITTINGHAM SNAPS

Benson, Frank. "Deliberate Murder Portrayed in Trial." *Marion Star,* August 29, 1973.

———. "Jury Faces 5 Choices in Shooting Case." *Marion Star,* August 31, 1973.

———. "Mrs. Whittingham Tells Jury of Fatal Night." *Marion Star,* August 30, 1973.

Hueslman, Neil, and Frank Benson. "Mrs. Whittingham Gets 2nd-Degree Murder Conviction." *Marion Star,* September 1, 1973.

Marion Star. "1st Degree Count Faced in Homicide." March 2, 1973.

———. "Life Sentence Given to Mrs. Whittingham." September 14, 1973.

———. "Murder Trial Gets Under Way." August 28, 1973.

THE PALACE THEATRE

Hall, Ben M. *The Best Remaining Seats: The Story of the Golden Age of the Movie Palace.* New York: C.N. Potter, 1961.

Looking Back: Historic Images of Marion County, Ohio. Vancouver, WA: Pediment Publishing, 2003.

Marion Palace Theatre. *Fast Facts about the Theatre.* Marion, Ohio, n.d.

Mayr, Bill. "Pride of Marion." *Columbus Dispatch,* October 24, 2004, section F.

With Unseen Hands

Carrington, Hereward. *Physical Phenomena of Spiritualism: Fraudulent and Genuine.* Boston, MA: Small, Maynard, & Co., 1908.

Conlin, Alexander. *The Life and Mysteries of the Celebrated Dr. "Q."* Los Angeles, CA: Alexander Publishing Company, 1921.

Cuffman, Jessica. "Woman Charged with Theft in Psychic Case." *Marion Star*, November 29, 2008, A3.

The History of Marion County, Ohio. Chicago, IL: Leggett, Conaway & Co., 1883.

Marion Daily Star. "Divine Services." January 23, 1896.

———. "They Materialized." March 6, 1896.

———. "With Unseen Hands." February 20, 1893.

White Lily Chapel. "About Us." http://www.whitelilychapel.org/About_Us.php.

———. "Who Is White Lily?" http://www.whitelilychapel.org/White_Lily.html.

The Nelson Street Haunting

Coshocton Tribune. "Girl Acquitted in Slaying of Father." July 1, 1960.

Hamilton Journal. "Girl, Acquitted of Slaying, Free." July 7, 1960.

Marion Star. "Napper a Tyrant, His Wife Declares." April 19, 1960.

———. "2 Daughters to Attend Napper Funeral Service." April 20, 1960.

Vance, William. "Girls Held in Father's Murder." *Marion Star*, April 18, 1960.

The Mongoloid House

Forgotten Ohio. "The Mongoid House." http://www.forgottenoh.com/Counties/Marion/mongoid.html.

Trains

Drake, David. "City Faces Passenger Train Loss." *Marion Star*, March 23, 1971.

Gerfen, Scott E. "Passenger Trains Were a Big Part of Marion's Past." *Marion Star*, July 12, 1998.

Harper, Gloria. "'Morbid Curiosity' Draws Onlookers." *Marion Star*, September 5, 1994.

Jacoby, John Wilbur, ed. *History of Marion County, Ohio, and Representative Citizens*. Chicago, IL: Biographical Pub. Co., 1907.

Lace, David. "Passenger Trains Nearing End of Line." *Marion Star*, March 28, 1970.

Marion Daily Star. "Dead Man's Valley." November 28, 1895.

Marion Star. "Freight Train Wreck at Union Station Kills Expressman and Smashes Building." February 28, 1949.

Marion Union Station Association. *Purpose of M.U.S.A.* Marion, Ohio, n.d.

Marion Weekly Star. "He Is Struck by an Engine." September 9, 1905.

Neidhardt, Carroll. *Ghost Stories, Mysteries & Things that Go Bump in the Night*. Marion, Ohio, 2007.

Parks, Richard. "The Cleveland Cincinnati Chicago and St. Louis Railroad (Big Four Route)." A Chicago Hub Railroad of the 1930s–1940s. http://www.r2parks.net/bigfour.html.

Scholz, David, and Gloria Harper. "Collision Leaves One Dead." *Marion Star*, August 28, 1994.

Slanser, Joe. "Railroad Transportation in Marion County." N.p, n.d.

The Marion Country Club Murder

Bishop, Jo. "Report Shows Huddle Died Violently." *Marion Star*, August 11, 1981.

California Department of Corrections. "Inmate Locator." http://inmatelocator.cdcr.ca.gov.

Danielsen, Margie. *Tainted Roses*. Far Hills, NJ: New Horizon Press, 2000.

Enfield, Bill. "Sacramento Rapist-Murderer Due Parole Hearing." September 3, 2010. http://blogs.sacbee.com/crime/archives/parole-hearing.

Keefe, Kevin J. "Local Law Officials Hope 'Parts' of Mack Will Tell Them Plenty." *Marion Star*, March 25, 1988.

———. "Tip from Marion County Leads to Arrest of Paul Mack in Utah." *Marion Star*, March 23, 1988.

Kirkus Reviews. Review of *Tainted Roses*, January 15, 2000. http://www.kirkusreviews.com/book-reviews/non-fiction/margie-danielsen/tainted-roses.

Lawlink.com. *People v. Mack*. 11 Cal.App.4th 1466, 15 Cal.Rptr.2d 193, 1992. http://www.lawlink.com/research/caselevel3/70024.

Marion Star. "Body of Woman Identified Today." July 15, 1981.

———. "Sheriff Probes Death." July 11, 1981.

———. "Woman's Body Found in River Saturday Remains Unidentified." July 13, 1981.

Taylor, Susie. "Sheriff Hopes Show on Huddle Case Fulfills Purpose." *Marion Star,* March 21, 1988.

MARION CAN BE A SCARY PLACE

Best, Joel, and Gerald T. Horiuchi. "The Razor Blade in the Apple: The Social Construction of Urban Legends." *Social Problems* 32, no. 5 (1985): 488–99.

Marion Independent. "The Olden Time in Marion." December 17, 1874.

Marion Star. "Marion Ghost Proves to be Sick Maid." March 22, 1922.

———. "Razor Blades Turn Up in Halloween Handouts." November 1, 1971.

Marion Weekly Star. "Slumbers of Boss Rudely Disturbed." October 23, 1909.

Santino, Jack. *Halloween and Other Festivals of Death and Life.* Knoxville: University of Tennessee Press, 1994.

MYSTERIOUS LIGHTS OVER HINAMON WOODS

The History of Marion County, Ohio. Chicago, IL: Leggett, Conaway & Co., 1883.

Howland, H.G. *Atlas of Marion County, Ohio.* Philadelphia, PA: Harrison, Sutton & Hare, 1878.

Marion Weekly Star. "Ghosts Appear, Some Think." September 4, 1905.

———. "Looking for the Strange Lights." September 9, 1905.

———. "The Mystery Increases." September 6, 1905.

A TRUE HORROR STORY

Bundick, Ahmed J. "End of Case Close at Hand." *Marion Star,* October 11, 1995.

Carter, Pamela D. "Deaths May be Homicide, Suicide." *Marion Star,* October 9, 1995.

———. "Police Outline Murder Scenario." *Marion Star,* October 10, 1995.

Lillis, Karen S. "Three Bodies Found in Silver Street Home." *Marion Star,* October 8, 1995.

HEADLESS HADDIE

Brooks, Jennifer. "Scout Camp Up for Bid." *Marion Star*, June 8, 1993.
Marion Star. "Scouts Open $400,000 Drive for New Camp." March 25, 1971.
Sankey, Mike. "Headless Haddie, English 270, Introduction to Folklore, Spring Quarter, 1975." Ohio State Folklore Archives, Columbus, Ohio.
Schneider, Nancy A., and William D. Ellis. *Yours in Scouting.* N.p.: Heart of Ohio Council Boy Scouts of America, 1997.

THE DOWNTOWN YMCA

Bolton, Roger, "City Police Lack Suspect, Weapon in YMCA Killing." *Marion Star*, August 22, 1974.
Goshert, Jake. "Out of Space, 'Y' to Leave Downtown." *Marion Star*, June 2, 1999.
Marion Star. "Grand Jury to Get Case of Y Slaying." September 10, 1974.
———. "Lampkin Plea Change Jolts Court, Jurors." January 14, 1975.
———. "Police Cite Robbery in 'Y' Murder." August 23, 1974.
———. "Toledo Man Arrested in 'Y' Slaying." August 30, 1974.

ODDS AND ENDS

Marion Daily Star. "Man at the Window." August 10, 1897.
———. "The Parkers Vacate the Haunted House." June 15, 1910.
Marion Republican. "Spooks and Witches." April 23, 1857.
Marion Star. "'Ghost' Car Reported Seen Near Prospect." N.d.
Myers, Charlton. *Tales from the Sage of Salt Rock of Marion County, Ohio.* Marion, OH: Audsam Printing Co., 1996.

ABOUT THE AUTHOR

Joshua Simpkins grew up in Marion, Ohio. He studied at the Ohio State University, receiving a BA in English in 1999 and an master's degree in education in 2000. He currently resides with his wife and small daughter in Bochum, Germany, where he works as an English instructor.

Visit us at
www.historypress.net